T0209857

WINNING AGAIN

HOPE FOR THE CHURCH IN LITTLE AMERICA

KEVIN VER HOEVEN

WESTBOW
PRESS®
A DIVISION OF THOMAS NELSON
& ZONDERVAN

WestBow Press books may be ordered through booksellers or by contacting:

WestBow Press
A Division of Thomas Nelson & Zondervan
1663 Liberty Drive
Bloomington, IN 47403
www.westbowpress.com
844-714-3454

Scripture quotations taken from The Holy Bible, New International Version® NIV® Copyright © 1973 1978 1984 2011 by Biblica, Inc. TM. Used by permission. All rights reserved worldwide.

ISBN: 978-1-6642-4028-5 (sc)
ISBN: 978-1-6642-4285-2 (hc)
ISBN: 978-1-6642-4027-8 (e)

Library of Congress Control Number: 2021914474

Print information available on the last page.

WestBow Press rev. date: 8/13/2021

CONTENTS

ACKNOWLEDGMENTS

I would like to thank the governor of my state for putting me in lockdown and keeping me in lockdown during the COVID-19 crisis. Because of your heavy hand, I have not had much more to do than write … and write … and write.

I also want to thank all the wonderful people I have been able cross paths with as I have served in "little" America. Your presence in my life has made my life rich, and my cup overflows with gratitude.

I also want to thank the council at the Bethel Christian Reformed Church. Because you saw the importance of sabbatical, I have had a great opportunity to rest, read, rejuvenate, and write.

And finally, I want to thank Suzanne, my best friend and amazing wife. You have left me alone to write even when you would have preferred that I help you plant flowers, wash windows, and paint. I love you with everything I could ever love you with.

A "LITTLE" BACKGROUND

I am not one to boast, but I can unequivocally and proudly tell you that I am an expert on "little." I was not born with this great wisdom, but rather this almost infinite wisdom has been forged through a lifelong journey of being a part of "little." For any big thing you can toss out to convince someone that you know more about "little" than I do, I can throw out something far "littler." Do not believe me? Try this "little" sampling of my life on for size, and you will see that for all your smalls, I am an extra small.

Let us begin with my stature. I did not come into this world all that small—a little over six pounds and about nineteen inches—but until my senior year in high school, that was the only time in my childhood that I was normal size. I was always the shortest boy in my class, and it really was not much of a competition. By the time I was a junior in high school, I was a doorway-scraping five feet two inches tall and a scale-breaking 110 pounds. When my wife first saw my junior picture, she thought for sure it was my seventh-grade picture … and she was being gracious with that assessment.

Now, for terms of full disclosure, not everything about me was small. For one, my mouth was big. This is probably because my mouth was used more than any other part of my body. I was never going to get anywhere with my physical attributes, so being a good steward of the gifts God had given me, I tried to be a good steward of my vocal attributes. Theologically, that may have been a sound decision, but practically, it was a disaster. In first grade, when the teacher made the comment that our class wasn't reading out loud very well that day, I chimed in with my astute observation that the reason for that was because she was "picking on all the bad readers in the class." If my memory serves me correctly, I enjoyed the next number of recesses playing by myself.

I was also privileged to have a younger brother who was considerably bigger than I was. I also had the privilege to have a younger brother with whom I did not get along very well and who, in my opinion, was a much worse sinner than I was or that I could ever see myself becoming. I also had the privilege of having a younger brother who had a bad temper. I do not know if any of you know this, but it is ridiculously hard to try to present your case when you are wrestling on the ground and you are the one with your back on the ground.

Still, all was not lost. I also had a younger brother with whom I shared a bedroom, and it was there, after the lights were off and the blankets were pulled up, that I honed the preaching skills that I still use today. My brother learned at an early age that falling asleep as soon as your head hits the pillow is one of life's greatest blessings.

I not only had a big mouth growing up, but I also, as I found out at a church camp I attended when I was about nine, had big lips. It just so happened that the camp I attended was also being attended by a group of guys from a nearby town. It also just so happened that these guys and I ended up in the same cabin and in the same basketball group. I never knew my lips were out of proportion to the rest of my face until these guys were kind enough to tell me … over and over and repeatedly.

I started my week at camp with the name of Kevin, and by the end of week, my name had changed to "Big Lips." It did not matter that I schooled them on the basketball court or that I knew my Bible better than they did; what mattered was that my self-esteem was beat up. Many will say that church camp is a great experience, and for many it is, but for me, it left a scar that lasted until the size of my face caught up with the size of my lips, which probably wasn't until my senior year of high school when my body finally started growing.

But my vast knowledge of "little" is not confined to my childhood body. I also grew up in a "little" town of just over seven hundred people. In that little town was a little church of about forty people that our family attended whenever the doors were open, which seemed like an awful lot. In that little community with the little church was also a rather little school I attended and then graduated from with a class of ninety-three. From that little town, I then went on to a little liberal arts college of about 1,200 students. It was there that I was able to play on the golf team, which was little, and with the little competition that was there, I was able to golf all four years.

During my junior year, I led a little Bible study in my dorm, and that led me to go into full-time ministry. After graduating from college, I attended a little seminary from which I eventually graduated and headed out into my first church in—you guessed it—a little community. The church wasn't little, but the community was just four corners with a few houses in the middle of cornfields. Five years later, I took a call to another church in—you guessed it—another little community, though by comparison, 1,500 people seemed like a major metropolitan area compared to where we were. From there, it was on to—you guessed it—another little community, this time of about 500 people. From there, I was led to plant a new church in—you did not guess it—a larger community in the northwest.

When that venture ended, I headed back to my home state of Michigan and served two churches in—you guessed it—little communities. And now for the last six plus years, I have served a church in—you guessed it—another little community.

So, when I say that I am an expert on "little," I am not kidding. Outside of four years of my life, I have been immersed in "little" America. In all these years, I learned a lot about the ins and outs and pluses and minuses of being a part of "little" America. So maybe, just maybe, I can share some wisdom about the role that little churches in little towns can have in the kingdom of God. My story is one of inconsistencies among the consistent. My story is not necessarily one of success but of survival. My story is not about a lot of great things that have happened but simply about a lot of things. Still, with all my experience in little places, this book is not so much about what has been but about what can be.

The writing of this book was precipitated by a change that took place in my life in the past year. In the past year, I realized that I have devoted too much time to doing pastoral things that haven't had a great impact on the kingdom of God and too little time doing the "Christian" thing that will have an impact for eternity. You are meeting me right now as I am making the transition from being a generic pastor to being a disciple-making pastor. I write this book not from a mind-set of telling you everything I know but from a mind-set of wishing I had started going in this direction a long time ago. As you read this book, we will be making footprints together as opposed to me asking you to step in the footprints I have already made. I trust that the little time you spend reading this book will have a big effect on your life and the kingdom of God. There is a path blazed by our Lord and Savior, Jesus Christ, that, if followed, will lead to the church in little America winning in the twenty-first century.

The issues raised in this book are not issues that are necessarily unique to little America, but they are issues that are prevalent in little America. If you are a Christian living in a community of less than four thousand, this is a book for you. This is a book that you can use as your inspiration to be the one to make a difference not only in the church in little America but in the kingdom of God. If you are a church board in little America, this is a book for you. This is a book that you can study together, reflect on together, and hopefully use to unite with other churches to not only make an impact on your community but on the kingdom of God. And, finally, if you a pastor in little America, this is a book for you. This book will not add another task to your already busy schedule. Rather it is a book that will give you hope that if there is a grassroots movement in your community to make disciples who make more disciples, then you will see that pastoring in little America can be a big, exciting adventure where we are not just conquerors but super-conquerors.

A "LITTLE" DREAM

I use the term *little dream* here not to describe the importance of the dream but to describe more its length. Imagine, if you will, the following picture. It is early Wednesday morning at the "Gossip Bench" café in Littletown, USA. For a number of years, this had been a watering hole reserved pretty much for the senior citizens of Littletown, who would gather four or five mornings a week to drink their coffee, talk trash with the help, and temporarily solve the problems of the world before leaving to tackle the tasks of the day.

But now there is a different clientele in the café—not only today but a couple of other days a week as well. These groups of three or four are not bringing their newspapers but rather their Bibles. These people are not bringing their laments of what once was but their hopes of what might be. These people are not voicing their complaints but rather their prayers. These people are not lifelong friends but rather newfound brothers and sisters in the Lord. These people are not connected by their biological blood but by the blood of Christ.

The same phenomenon is happening at the new coffee shop on the other side of Littletown. Two to three afternoons a week, tables at A Whole Latte Coffee are populated by groups of three or four younger adults who have brought their iPhones and tablets and are busy discussing anything from how today's current events relate to the Bible to the newest teachings on how they can be better friends, husbands, wives, or parents. Like the groups at the Gossip Bench, the groups at A Whole Latte Coffee are not sharing tales of yesterday but are voicing their dreams for today and tomorrow. Like the groups at the Gossip Bench, the groups at A Whole Latte Coffee are not expressing their complaints but are articulating their prayers. Like the groups at the Gossip Bench, the groups at A Whole Latte Coffee are not connected by biological blood but by the blood of Jesus Christ.

And here is what is most amazing: these groups are made up of people not from the same church but from three or four different churches. Months ago, these people hardly even knew each other. Because of the dynamics of "little" America, they knew of each other. They were connected by knowing others who knew others that they knew. They were further connected by the Family Bingo cards identifying whose grandparents or aunts or uncles lived or worked with third, fourth, or fifth cousins,, but they didn't know each other.

For a long time, most of them had been traveling in the same spiritual rut. They had grown up in Littletown, and once they married, they either stayed in the church of their youth or made the major move to attending the church of their new spouse. Their participation in their church pretty much mirrored the participation of their parents and grandparents. If their parents were regular attenders, went to Sunday School, and served on committees or the board, they followed suit and did the same. If their parents missed church in the spring or fall to do farmwork or the summer to go camping, the next generation did the same. If their parents had quickly left after church to go to Grandma's for coffee and cookies, they now did the same.

Once in a while, a seismic shift happened when a new pastor who was a little more charismatic came into town or a pastor stayed in town too long and offended someone one too many times or a new family moved into town who had some money and thus were courted as royalty, but for the most part, people stayed at the same church. It was their home. It was a constant in an ever-changing world. It was a scheduled place for grandparents to see their grandkids and for siblings to reconnect after seven days without their siblings. It was a safe place to engage in the things they enjoyed doing—singing, helping with vacation Bible school, sitting in the nursery, or helping to take care of the church building and its grounds.

For the most part, the people were content with this arrangement. There was the Dutch church and the German church and the Railroad church and the Free Will church and the Calvinist church. They had their monikers, and they didn't mind one bit. This was part of their identity, part of who they were in Littletown.

On the surface, all seemed peaceful and civil. Each church did their own thing, and everyone got along. But the dirty little secret was that all was not peaceful, and everyone didn't get along. The number of churches in Littletown was disproportionate to the size of the town. In a town of 1,800, there were six churches in the city limits and a couple more country churches just on the outskirts. Originally, there had been three churches, but through the years, the number had increased for reasons no one really knew anymore, and you weren't going to find out unless you were naïve enough to start asking a lot of questions. Of the six churches in town, four of them averaged less than fifty in worship, another one averaged seventy-five, and then there was the church "that was stealing sheep" and was averaging 150. The largest "church" in town was the group of residents who used to attend one of these churches but had since dropped out and now did not go anywhere.

And the numbers had been dwindling. The old people were dying, and the young people were leaving, so if a church was maintaining, it was really growing. The churches were doing all they could to survive, leaving little energy for new ministries, programs, or community initiatives. No wonder then that when one of the churches became vacant, the church had a hard time finding someone to come and be their pastor.

But that was four years ago. No one can really explain why things started changing or who exactly got the ball rolling, but a spiritual revival gradually took place in Littletown. Some wanted to give credit to the new pastor at the German church, while others argued that it really started at the Railroad church with a couple of religious fanatics. No one really noticed anything for a couple of years, and still today, many are not seeing anything, but for many, this something was real, and this something was transforming their lives and their churches.

The truth of the matter is that this spiritual awakening was not started by one of the local pastors, nor was it started by any decisions of any of the local church boards. The awakening started in the prayer closet of a couple who were lifelong residents of Littletown and were one day convicted of the ineffectiveness and fruitlessness of the churches in their community. This couple did not make a prayer request for anything at their church's morning service the next week, nor did they go and talk to their pastor about how they were feeling, nor did they talk to any of their friends. They simply talked to God and asked God for confirmation that this uneasiness had come from him and then direction for how they should proceed.

What they heard God say to them was for them to fast and pray for the next month and listen to the voice of God and that if they would humble themselves before Him, he would reveal what needed to be done to bring about a spiritual breakthrough in Littletown. The couple were obedient, but what they heard did not seem to make a lot of sense at the time. What God revealed to them was that each of them needed to find a couple of people from the other churches in town to join them in a weekly time of sharing and connecting in the Word of God. But they were to go slowly. Before they talked to anyone, they were to pray and fast for another month, asking God to reveal who those people were, and God would be speaking to those people in the time being.

And that is how the spiritual revival in Littletown took root. The couple did as God commanded, and as they prayed and fasted that month, God kept setting Matthew 28:18–20 in front of them: "Go and make disciples of all nations baptizing them in the name of the Father and the Son and the Holy Spirit and I will be with you always." That was it! Why, they wondered, had they missed this for so long? The key to effectiveness and fruitfulness in the church was not better programming or better preaching or better fellowship; the key was carrying out the Great Commission. The truth was that they had known these verses all their lives, but they had never understood the application and practicality of the verses.

At the end of the two months, God had placed five people each on the hearts of the couple. It was time to go and ask the question. They headed out to talk to these people with some trepidation but trusting they were doing what God wanted them to do. Their mission? To ask each of these people if they would be interested in getting together once a week for three months to open the Bible and their lives with each other and then go from there. It was not a surprise to the husband, but still affirming, to hear three of the five he asked say, "Now I know what God was up to with me in the past month. I don't know what this is about or exactly what I am doing, but when God persistently knocks on the door of my heart, I can't say no."

The wife had the same response with two of the five women she asked. They had no idea where they were going or why, but they knew the hand of God was in it, and, like with Abraham, God was going to get them to the land he was not identifying at the moment.

And so the journey began. The next week, the couple met with their people at the Gossip Bench at different times, and they simply shared. They didn't bring their Bibles, and they didn't bring any books, but they brought their stories, and they brought their lives. They shared what God had been doing in their lives and what they felt God might be wanting to do in their lives now. They shared significant moments from their pasts, nothing real deep but more than they would have shared in a social setting. And when their hour together was over, they felt something inside of them that they had not felt for a long time, if ever. It was hard to explain, but it was something that said, "This is worthwhile, this is important, and I won't be doing life the way I've been doing it ever again."

They met again the next week and the next week and the week after. With each progressing week, they shared more deeply, studied more diligently, and searched for God's leading more decisively. Soon, they realized that what they had needed to be shared with others. They started praying and fasting, asking God whom they should take along with them and how they should divide. After three months, John's original group of four was splitting into three groups of three, and Marilyn's original group of three was splitting into two groups of four.

We now fast-forward four years. The Christians in Littletown are still not where they want to be, but they have made great progress. Instead of having the Dutch church and the German church and the Free Will church and the Railroad church, they now really have one church: "Christ's church." They still meet in different buildings and have their own worship styles and some of their own activities. All of them still have their own personalities. But now when they are asked what church they attend, they ponder the question for a moment and then answer, "The only church in town. The church that is striving to make disciples who make disciples." They are no longer divided by their pasts or by their apologetics. Through a few years of sharing life together, they have agreed that doctrinal differences will no longer divide them but that they will be unified and energized by the words of the Apostle's Creed:

> I believe in God the Father almighty, maker of the heaven and the earth. And in Jesus Christ his only begotten Son our Lord. Who was born of the virgin Mary, suffered under Pontius Pilate, was crucified dead and buried. He descended into hell. The third day he rose again and sits on the right hand of God the Father from thence he shall come to judge the living and the dead. I believe in the Holy Christian Church, the communion of saints, the forgiveness of sin, the resurrection of the body and the life everlasting. Amen.

And now the largest "church" in Littletown is no longer the church of the formerly churched but the church of the Great Commission. Now there are groups of three and four meeting at all the local restaurants several times a week. Now when there are people to help and things to be done in the community, these groups are out combining their forces to help in whatever way they can. Now people who had no interest in Jesus Christ are on the front lines sharing their faith by word and deed. Now there are groups of ten to twelve meeting in homes, sharing their stories, studying the story of the Bible, and getting ready to go out and share the good news with whomever they may meet wherever they may go.

The remaining chapters will explain how this dream can become a reality. They will explain how churches in "little" America can be invigorated and impact the kingdom of God in ways none of us have seen in our lifetimes. If this is your dream and if you believe our God is big enough to make the dream come true, keep reading, and take this journey with me.

A "LITTLE" CRITIQUE

TOO LITTLE REPENTANCE

I have spent all my life, save nine months, in the reformed corner of the Protestant room. That being the case, I learned at an early age that the confession of sin is the first step we take before we move forward. The order of worship that I grew up with, and was then taught in seminary, included a section at the beginning of the service when there would be a corporate confession of our sin, followed by some words from scripture assuring us of the forgiveness of those sins, and then a time when we would read the law, or the Ten Commandments with the idea of showing us how to live. I have since come to believe that the law was given to show us how live in gratitude for our deliverance from sin. This was done at the beginning of the service, following the opening hymn as part of the section of the worship service that fell under the heading of "Our Approach to God."

While I sometimes found this part of the worship service to be rather dry and wooden, I do believe in the theology of this framework, not only for worship but for all of life. Our God desires above all else a "broken and contrite heart" because that is the heart that God molds and shapes and uses. So if the church in little America is going to be reinvigorated, it will start with hearts that are reinvigorated. That happens when we confess that we have been missing the mark, that we have fallen short of the glory of God, and that we have not been the children that God the Father has wanted us to be.

So we are going to corporately, and hopefully individually, confess some of the sins of little America. It has been my experience in my families, both biological and church, that we have no problem confessing our sins if we don't have to be too specific when we do so. Far too often around the kitchen table and from the pulpit, I have heard the generic, "Forgive us our sins, Lord," with no hesitation before moving on to the next lines of the prayer. We are not going to do that. This is not going to be a generic confession of sin. This is going to be a confession of specific sin.

We start by confessing to the sin of *legalism*. Though it has become less prevalent recently, this sin has pretty much always been a part of the fabric of the "little" places I have been. It has also been my experience that this sin is flaunted more than it is camouflaged. Listen closely, and this sin is announced far and wide. See if any of these phrases do not ring a bell or resonate with you. "The real Christians are the ones who not only worship on Sunday morning but are also there on Sunday night." "Real Christians don't mow their lawns or wash their cars or hang out their laundry on Sundays." This one may be a little outdated, but when we moved to one of our small towns, the TV antenna was in the attic. My dad saw that and commented, "Oh, that's a Christian Reformed Church antenna." The reasoning was that "Real Christians don't watch TV."

Or how about these? "Real Christians don't go into the bar," or "Real Christians don't smoke, and if they do, they only do so in designated places outside the church," or "Real

Christians don't date anyone who doesn't attend another one of the churches in town," or "Real Christians don't wear blue jeans to church," or "Real Christians don't hang out with non-Christians," or "Real Christians don't golf on Sundays or let their kids play any club sports on Sundays," or "Real Christians aren't Republicans," or Real Christians aren't Democrats."

I am writing this in the middle of the COVID-19 lockdown. Some of our governors have made up some rules I know are not based on scientific data. A couple that are most questionable to me are you can drive your car with your family of four inside of it and your boat behind it to the lake, but once you get to the lake and put your boat in the water, only two people can be in the boat. I'm going out on a limb here, but I am predicting that there will never be scientific data to support this rule. The other one concerns the beaches in California. People can now be on the beaches if they are running, playing games, or doing some kind of physical exercise, but they cannot be on the beach if they are only sitting or on a beach chair. In fact, they cannot be on the beach if they are standing still. Unless, of course, if they are fishing while they are standing still, and then they can be on the beach. Once again, I do not claim to be a scientist, but I doubt if there will ever be any scientific data to support this rule.

We hear about these rules, and we scratch our heads as to their reasonableness or feasibleness. But at the same time, little America is notorious for coming up with their own spiritual laws that cannot be supported and validated by scripture. So we need to repent of our spirit of legalism.

The second sin we need to confess is the sin that is on the opposite side of the coin with legalism. That sin is *permissiveness*. On this side of the coin, we find a plethora of sins that are not only tolerated but ignored in little America. Perhaps the most obvious is the sin of *gossip*. We cloak this under the rug of the church prayer chain. But just because we pass a juicy morsel along via a prayer chain doesn't mean that many people aren't using the prayer chain as their vehicle for finding things to gossip about. If you don't think that gossip is overlooked in little America, let me ask you a question. In truth, the answer is probably the same in "big" America, but here it is. "When is the last time you can remember the church disciplining someone for gossip?" It never happens, and I am guilty of this. Not of gossip, because I only pass things along that concern me. But I have never gone into an elders' meeting and said to the elders, "We need to do something about so and so . Her gossiping ways are sucking the life out of this church right now."

We laugh at Yenta in *Fiddler on the Roof,* but the amount of gossip that is ignored in little America is not something to laugh about. Gossip is insidious and does unmeasurable damage to the body of Christ. I am not only talking about incorrect gossip that slides into slander. Why is it that little America seems to act like controlling the tongue is only an injunction for larger America? In little America, a loose tongue is not only acceptable but sometimes even lauded. Before we try to move forward, may we pause to repent of the sin of gossip.

A third sin we need to confess is that of *stereotyping*. I could share several stories here, but this one has stuck with me the longest. In one of the small towns I served, there was a young man who had been a rebel in high school. If there was anything wrong that he could have done, he did it. If there was anything he could have done to make life miserable for others, he did it. If there was anything he could have said that would have ticked people off, he said it. And then he went off to a Christian college and found the Lord. He did a one-eighty and came back to his hometown a changed person. His faith was obvious. His transformation was contagious. His story was compelling. I was serving a church that couldn't afford any additional staff, so when he expressed some interest in helping me, I jumped at the offer. But I let him know it would have to be as a volunteer. He was unfazed. "I just love the Lord, and I want to serve him however I can," was his response.

His idea was to start a Sunday evening contemporary service a couple of Sunday nights a month. He played guitar and sang. He knew a drummer and a couple other musicians in the area who would help lead the service. The board gave their approval, and so the venture began. It did not last long, but there were a few great services. At one point, this young man asked if he could do the service in the morning to give people a taste of what was happening at night. This is where it got a little dicey—not because of the style of worship but because of his past. As we were trying to sell the idea, one of the board members said something like, "I don't think we should do this. Remember, this kid was terrible when he was in high school, and I don't think he should be up front leading us on Sunday morning."

My experience has told me this is not a once-in-the-history-of-the-church-of-little-America moment. It happens way too often. We should not be surprised or dismissive of this. Do you remember what was said of Jesus of Nazareth? "What good could ever come out of Nazareth?" What would prompt such a question? The same thing that prompted the comment from that board member. When you are known one way as a kid or when a small town is known one way by others, stereotypes are hard to break. Through the years, I have had guys tell me that they have given up putting up their names for leadership positions in the church because of their past—not because they don't believe God has forgiven them but because they don't have any evidence that the "life-timers" of the community or church have forgiven them for who they were as teenagers or what happened in a previous marriage or a previous business venture.

The good news is that in little America, we are known by the other people in town. The bad news in that in little America, we are known by the other people in town. When we are known by others, it is easy for stigmas to be attached to us: the adulterer, the divorcée, the rebel, the guy from the wrong side of the tracks, the mother who is a thorn in the side of the teachers, the family who teaches their kids some weird ideas, the gal who is accused of being a peeping Tam. I wonder how many people in little America have never been what God wanted them to be, how many people could have been catalysts for the kingdom, because they couldn't break through the stereotypes cast on them by the residents of their small town. Before we stifle anyone else, we need to repent of the sin of stereotyping.

The fourth sin we need to confess is the sin of *unfriendliness*. Believe me. I can hear your rebuttal from all over little America, but I stand by my statement. I know that when small churches in small towns are asked, "What is the strength of your church?" the most common answer is that we are a friendly church. To which the following question needs to then be asked, "Friendly to whom?" For the most part, I don't believe people in little America are intentionally unfriendly, but I believe that because most people in little America have lived in their little town for most of their life and because they are known by others they don't really understand what it is like to come into a gathering and feel all alone because they don't know anybody. Because we haven't sat in the seat of the unknown person, we don't realize how meaningful it is to that person when someone comes up and starts talking to him or her.

Here are some of examples of unfriendliness I have seen and experienced. When I was in college, a group of us attended a local church on most Sundays. There is one person I remember from that church more than any other (in fact, he is the only person I remember). Why do I remember him? When he would come up and welcome us, he would shake our hands, which was nice, but as he did, he would be looking everywhere in the church except at us. Now, how do you think that made us feel? Important? Welcome? How about insignificant compared to everyone else in the building? I think he thought he was being friendly, but his wandering eyes said otherwise.

Here is another one, or ones, because it is a regular occurrence in churches. The service is over and people are gathering in their groups—er, cliques. It is the same arrangement every week. This family here. That family there. These friends here. Those friends there. And conspicuously noticeable to me is the person or couple who has just started attending the church. Whom are they standing or sitting with? No one. The time before and after the service is often the loneliest time for people who are visiting our church or who have not yet been assimilated into the life of the church. We would never say we are unfriendly to visitors and outsiders, but what do our actions say? The leaders of the church can make continual reminders to be friendly to "everyone," but the truth is that only a few really make an effort to make people outside our clique, or group, feel welcome.

Here is another one. When I started at one of my churches, I noticed a man sitting in the back of the sanctuary all by himself. He didn't come at the last minute, but he did leave right after the service, even before I got a chance to introduce myself to him. After about a month, I started asking a few of the regulars who this guy was. What I heard from them was, "Well, he started coming here a couple of months ago, but we don't know his name." And yet I had been told in my interview that this was a friendly church. Really? How could someone come to a church of less than fifty people for a few months and have no one come up to him and find out who he was. The neat ending to his story is that this man stayed with us and eventually became the man who invited more people than anyone else to come to our church (and some people deny the grace of God).

I finish with a couple of the more egregious example of unfriendliness—egregious because the unfriendliness was not a matter of ignorance or naïveté but out of hostility. The first became apparent to me after I had been at a place for some time. I noticed that there were certain people who never talked to other people. In fact, I noticed, they did not even sit near each other in the sanctuary. At first, that didn't faze me because through the years churches have undesignated designated seating. But finally the Holy Spirit led me to ask one of the trusted leaders in the church if I was imagining things or if there was really something going on. It was not my imagination. There had been a spat in the past between these people. It had been so long ago that the leader could not really remember what it was about. And since that time, these individuals stopped talking to each other.

The other example is worse. A town was going through the pain of having to consolidate school districts, and the effect was the reenactment of the Civil War in the middle of little America. Sides were drawn, words were shared, and doing what Jesus would do was forgotten all about. One Sunday, one of the teachers in town who was on one of the sides visited our church. I was thrilled to see him and his family. They did not normally attend church, and I sensed they were pulled by the Holy Spirit into our place that morning. In my enthusiasm, I said something to one of the people in the building, and I was not ready for the vitriolic response. I could not believe how a churchgoer could care so little for the soul of an unsaved person. I thank the Lord that this has been the only time I have ever see such venom be directed at a person by someone who claimed to be a Christian.

We need to be honest. Whether intentionally or unintentionally, little America does not have a corner on the market of friendliness, and if the church in little America is going to win, we need to confess our unfriendliness and start acting more like Jesus. I am qualified to say this because I am an introvert. I used to use that as an excuse for being unfriendly, but there are no excuses for unfriendliness. Friendliness is commanded not suggested. Friendliness is for everyone not just extroverts.

I preface the fifth sin we need to confess by saying that many will deny this and many more will not like me for bringing this up. We need to confess to *idolatry* in that we often act as if we love our families more than we love God. The first commandment is that we are not to have any other gods before God because God is a jealous God. You are going to think I have had nothing but bad experiences serving churches in little America, which is not the truth at all, but the stories I tell are part of the full picture or what I've learned. Here is another of those stories. It was the first Sunday in June. In the church I was at, Communion was always served on the first Sunday of the month. There were four elders in this church, and at this time, two of them were from the same family. As you know, early June is graduation time, and one of these men had a son who was graduating from high school. For whatever reason, the open house for this boy was scheduled for a Sunday morning. When I got the invitation to attend, I knew one thing: I wasn't going to be able to attend because it ran at the same time I had pastor responsibilities. I also knew that we might be short of elders to serve Communion, but the policy was that if an elder couldn't be there, he or she would find a replacement.

On the Saturday night before the service, I got a frantic call from the elder who had planned his son's open house for the following morning. "I just remembered we have Communion tomorrow morning and me and my brother-in-law won't be able to be there. Can you find someone to fill in for us?"

With great effort, I held my tongue, and I said I would take care of it.

I love family. I cherish the times my wife and I can see our kids and the times we can be with siblings and the times I can still be with my parents, and I have the most adorable grandson in the whole world. I also realize how easy it is for my love for my family to supersede my love for the Lord. I realize how easy it is for me to give more attention to my family than to God. I am aware of how natural it is for me to think about my family more than about God. When I say we need to repent of the sin of loving family more than God, I am with all of you in that boat.

But just because a pastor struggles with this sin does not mean that it is okay for us to disobey God when he tells us he needs to be our first love. I have never had someone come up and tell me, "Pastor, I confess I love my family more than God," and I do not think I ever will. But as John says in 1 John 3:18 (NIV), "let us not love with words but with actions." What is the proof that we love God more than our families? We put him first. We spend more time with him. We think about him more than anyone else. His commands take precedence over the commands and expectations our families put on us.

But if we take an honest look at how things go in little America, we must at least wonder if we love God more than family. When family gatherings continually come first over church events, what does that say? When we do not have time to serve on teams because we are too busy going to our kids' or grandkids' activities, what does that say? When we have no interest in being in discipleship groups or life groups because we have our own families, what does that say? When our grandchildren get our tithe and the church doesn't, what does that say?

I realize this sin is a slippery one to get a handle on. I realize that loving God and loving family is not an either/or matter. I realize that our families need to be loved and that we need to spend time with our families. I realize that being a good parent is being there to watch our kids in their activities or to coach our kids on their teams. I realize that family memories and traditions are made when milestones are celebrated together as families. But I also realize that we need to be careful with this one because of how easy it is to put our love for our families before our love for God. Navigating this challenge is hard, but we need to remember that the very nature of families is the multiple generations involved. What are we teaching the next by our actions? What is the next generation catching by what they see?

Jesus knew that navigating this fine line of loving family and loving God was difficult. That is why he addressed it forcefully with a challenge to all of us to decide which we were going to love more because loving both the same wasn't going to work. When Jesus said in Luke 14:26 (NIV), "If anyone comes to me and does not hate father and mother, wife and children, brothers and sisters—yes, even their own life—such a person cannot be my disciple," did he really mean hate? I hardly think so. So, what did he mean? I believe he meant love me so much that your family will have no doubt that I am your first love. This may not be easy to admit or to feel conviction for, but if the church in little America is to be invigorated, we much confess that we are guilty at times of loving family more than God.

2

TOO LITTLE GOD

One of the favorite stories I have used in sermons is the story of a new bar being built in a small town. The story goes like this: In a small Texas town (Mt. Vernon), Drummond's Bar began construction on a new building to increase their business. The local Baptist church started a campaign to block the bar from opening with petitions and prayers.

Work progressed right up until the week before opening when lightning struck the bar, and it burned to the ground. The church folks were rather smug in their outlook after that, until the bar owner sued the church on the grounds that the church was ultimately responsible for the demise of his building, either through direct or indirect actions or means. The church vehemently denied all responsibility or any connection to the building's demise in its reply to the court.

As the case made its way into court, the judge looked over the paperwork. At the hearing, he commented, "I don't know how I'm going to decide this case. It appears that we have a bar owner who believes in the power of prayer and an entire church congregation that does not."

This story is a story about prayer, but it is also a story about the size of God. When I title this chapter "Too Little God," I do not mean we have been getting too little of God, but rather that "little" America has a God who is too little. Our minds are amazing things, both for good and for bad. In regard to the size of God in little America, I think we have been duped by our surroundings to believe that the size of God changes to correspond to the size of our area. Let me explain. I have always considered myself to be a believer in God. I have also always believed that God is bigger than all my problems and fears. I have also always believed that God is all-powerful and that he can do anything he wants to do. I have also wished to see God act as that great big God that I believe him to be. When I hear about people talk of the great and miraculous things that God has done in their lives or their family or their community, I generally feel rather left out. I have no problem sharing stories of the presence of God or the providence of God or the grace of God or the mercy of God or the justice of God, but I just haven't had many times in my life when I have witnessed the power of God in a human life.

There can be several reasons for this. It can be that my faith is not strong enough. It can be that my analytical mind, which tries to figure everything out, has not left room for things to happen that cannot be figured out or that cannot be explained with logic and reason. And it may be that all my time living in little places has had the effect of leading me to subconsciously think little.

For the most part, visionaries and big thinkers do not thrive in little America. A big thinker is always asking, "How can we do this better?" People in little America generally ask, "What can we do to get this to work the way it used to work?" A big thinker asks, "What is out there that we aren't seeing?" People in little America generally ask, "Why aren't we able to see what is here as clearly as we used to?" A big thinker asks, "What can we concoct to get over this hurdle?" People in little American generally ask, "What can we do to make life more comfortable on this side of the hurdle?" Big thinkers ask, "What must we do to win?" People in little America generally ask, "What must we do to not lose?"

Another factor in little America that programs us to think small is that not much changes in small towns. Road construction draws a crowd. The arrival of a new minister gets on the front page of the weekly newspaper. The exploits of a local team warrant a police car and firetruck escort back into town. The closing or opening of a business is the talk in the coffee shop. A committed crime is all over town almost before it is on the scanner page. There is a routine and rhythm in little America that normalizes a mind-set that expects extraordinarily little out of the ordinary to ever happen.

What happens in little America is that our circumstances have a way of pushing us into a surviving mode rather than a thriving mode, and when we are focused on merely surviving, we stop dreaming of what can be and start hoping that if we can just keep doing the same things a little better, we can get through this. The effect is that we think small. We think maintenance rather than expansion. We think comfort rather than adventure. We think safety rather than ingenuity. We think that the best day on a boat is a calm day so we will not capsize rather than a windy day that can blow us forward on an exciting ride to a different destination.

And this safe, logical, reasonable, analytical, cautious approach to life eventually invades our spiritual lives, and with this attitude, our expectations of God are lowered to the point that if he keeps us healthy or employed or clothed or fed or sheltered or comfortable or understood or at peace, then we have a great big God. But size is relative, isn't it? I look huge to my grandson, but to some of the guys in my church or the kids on my golf team, I am a midget. I truly believe we think we see God as big, but our actions and decisions say otherwise.

A couple of years ago, I was challenged as to how big I believed God really was. My wife and I have been a part of a freedom ministry for the past three years. Our involvement in this ministry was precipitated by experiences we have had with our youngest child, whom we adopted internationally when he was younger than three years old. When we got our son, he was emotionally wounded. The first two and half years of his life were hard on him. He had been neglected. He had been abandoned. He may have been abused. And he most certainly had been imprisoned by Satan.

I never had a class in seminary on spiritual warfare, and both my wife and I were brought up in stable homes so we really weren't all that acquainted with the wounds that can be inflicted on people in their childhood. That all changed with our son. We now know more about spiritual warfare and woundedness than we would ever want. But while we had learned a lot, there was still so much we didn't know, and there was a yearning inside us to be able to help others who were wounded and in bondage. Another couple in our town was traveling down a parallel path to ours, and by the grace of God, he connected our paths and then led us to connect with a ministry an hour from us called "Wellsprings of Freedom International." Wellsprings is a ministry designed to set people free from their past hurts and wounds. We took the ten-week orientation class, and each week, we were introduced to people who had amazing stories to tell about the "big" God who had delivered them from bondage to Satan and who were now experiencing joy and peace and love like they had never experienced before in their lives.

I was inspired, intrigued, and conflicted. I had never known people who were so changed by their "big" God. I really wondered how this could be so real. I believe in the Holy Spirit, even though the denomination I grew up in emphasized God the Father and God the Son more than God the Spirit, but I had never seen God do such miraculous work ... and on such a consistent basis. It was enough for me to visit with the leaders of this ministry and tell them about my spiritual wrestling match. I wanted to be part of this. I wanted to be part of something that was truly transforming lives. I was tired of meeting with hurting people, having prayer with them, and then watching them head out the door to continue their life of quiet desperation.

In my visit with these godly men, I realized that I needed to be delivered from the demons of unbelief and doubt and religion and logic. Up to that moment, I did not know that I was being oppressed by the Evil One. I thought it was natural and normal and okay for me feel about God the way that I did. But after meeting with these men, I realized that my many years of living in "little" America had made me oblivious to the foothold Satan had gotten in my life. It was not the fault of the communities that I had lived in. They were not to blame. They had not been my oppressors. But my continual exposure to "little" had affected me to the point that even my God had become little. My eyes were opened to see that God was much bigger than I had been seeing him and, even worse, that I had been leading the members of my churches to see him.

I am glad to report that with the help of Wellsprings, I am now on a journey where my God is getting bigger and bigger all the time. Seeing the miraculous is becoming more of the norm than the exception. Hearing the unexplainable is becoming a common occurrence. Feeling the indescribable is becoming a habit.

I am now a team leader for a freedom ministry in our little town. The ministry has not taken off in the big way that we have hoped, but our big God is doing big things in the people who admit they need help and who are taking advantage of this ministry. It is such a rush to see the same people who walked in with their feet and spirits dragging leave with spirits soaring and their feet bouncing. We take no credit for this transformation. To stay humble and to focus all the attention on our great big God, we begin every session with a prayer that goes something like this:

> O Lord, we ask that this room may be filled with your Holy Spirit. We ask that this room may be considered holy ground. We know that great things are going happen here not because of us but because freedom can only happen through the power and authority of Jesus Christ. We know we will encounter opposition today so, in the name of Jesus, we remind all you demons that Jesus is the Son of man and that all of you have been defeated by Him. Almighty God, we ask that you place the blood covering of Jesus over everyone in this room including their family and friends. We forbid all demons from manifesting at any time during this session. And, Lord, we ask you to elevate the spiritual gifts of everyone in this room and to provide the team with all the authority necessary to complete this session. We finish by commanding all blocking, distracting, and interfering spirits to be cut off from everyone in this room and sent to the feet of Jesus. *Amen.*

After the prayer, we enter the courts of God with praise music and then we let God be God. It is amazing for all of us. And now, for the about the first time in my life, I have received visual evidence that our God is bigger than employment, shelter, food, clothing, comfort, or peace. Our God is a God of miracles, and that miracle-working God does not only do his work in "bigger" America, he also does his work in "little" America. And this is what is so mind-boggling about this: he has chosen each of us to be the lens through which people can see how big God is. Remember what Jesus said as he was getting ready to leave his disciples? "Very truly I tell you, whoever believes in me will do the works I have been doing, and they will do even greater things than these, because I am going to the Father" (John 14:12 NIV). Why could Jesus make such a statement? Not because us "little" people are so great but because we serve the same great big God that Jesus, God's only begotten son, served. We have been given the power, in the name of Jesus, to bind and loose. We have been given power, in the name of Jesus. to set the prisoners free. We have been given the power, in the name of Jesus, to bring sight to the blind, hearing to the deaf, and speech to the mute.

And so, in each and every one of us who live in little America, God is also present in little America. I believe that God is just as jealous about and zealous for little America as he is about big America. I believe God is just as passionate about transformed lives in little America as he is in big America. I believe God is just as committed to building his kingdom in little America as he is in big America. If this is the case, and I know that it is, then we have to know that God is not only going to give a little bit of himself to us but that he is going to give us all of who he is. We must never get lured into believing that just because we live in a little place that we have a little God.

3

TOO LITTLE HOPE

A few years ago, I did something that definitely wasn't on my bucket list. I know what your response is to this: "So, what! I do a lot of things that are not on my bucket list." I agree with your response, but this exception to doing something that was not on my bucket list was out of character for me. You see, I do not like to travel outside the country. There are several reasons for this, including a weak stomach, but what it boils down to is that I am not that adventurous. When I travel, I prefer to go to places where I will be comfortable. I prefer to go to places where I won't be worrying about the traffic, the crime, or the cultural and language differences. So usually when I go away, I go to … little places in little spots around the country. I like the backroads. I like the solitude. I like to slow down and gaze at the majesty of God's creation. I prefer the sound of crickets to that of semis roaring as I lay down for the night.

This being my nature, it was a surprise to me that I ended up in Haiti. Why? Well, that was the question I asked myself all the way up to my trip and all during my trip. Why? Before I give you my answer, I will give the cause. Our community has come to sort of adopt a young man from Haiti. This young man grew up in Haiti until he became sick. He was then brought to the United States, where he was raised by a loving American man and woman. But his heart never left Haiti, and upon graduating from college, he felt the calling to go back to Haiti and help his homeland. This young man is one of the most impressive people I have ever been around in my life. He founded a Christian school in Haiti called Mission Starfish Haiti. Why Starfish? He once came across a starfish in distress and reached out to rescue that starfish. Those with him asked him why. There were so many starfish. They said, "There are so many you will never ever make in dent in helping all the starfish that need help." To which this young man replied, "But I can help this one." And thus began his dream to found a Christian school near his hometown in Haiti.

For two years, our community had been sending work groups down to Haiti to help at Mission Starfish. I never had an interest. As I said, I do not like leaving the comfortable for the uncomfortable; plus, I am not a real fan of doing manual labor. (Sometimes having a weak back can be advantageous.) However, being impressed with the man who had started the school, I said I would join the next group if he had a group of pastors he would like for me to train. He did! And I was on my way, getting ready to go all the while wondering why I was doing this and worrying what shape my stomach would be in while I was there.

The day came for our departure, and we reached the final leg of our flight. A jaunt from Ft. Lauderdale, Florida, to Port-au-Prince. I found my seat. I groaned a little as the seat was a middle seat, and I was separate from the rest of our group. *Oh well*, I thought, *a little time to catch a nap*. But that was not to be. The lady next to me started up a conversation, and before too long, with my prodding, she was telling me her story. She and her husband lived in the States, and her husband had a good job in the government. She was originally from Haiti and was now heading down to her hometown to investigate starting up a restaurant where she would teach the local residents how to cook and run a business. I was impressed and inspired. This lady had quite a dream and enough hope that if she did what she was dreaming, she could make a difference for a few people in her hometown. I put her story in my mental notebook as something to ponder and share when I returned home.

A couple of days into our stay, the founder of the school took us to meet a couple of his friends. These friends happened to be entrepreneurs from the States. They had started a little store where they sold products made by the locals in the city. The work of the locals was wonderful, but the tangible items they were selling paled in comparison to the dream they were pursuing. On their property was an old warehouse that they were rebuilding. There are very few grocery stores in Haiti, and in this community, people have to travel two hours to get to a grocery story that supplies all that they need. Seeing the need, this couple was in the process of converting this old warehouse into a grocery store. There was a long way to go, but this couple had a heart for the people of this community and a hope that through their efforts and resources, they could make a positive difference in the lives of the people there.

As the week ended, the founder of the school took us on another road trip. This time, he took us on a forty-five-minute ride to his hometown. This town was extremely poor. We parked the truck, and then our host led us on a walk to the back of the village. There at the back of village were sixty acres of untilled farmland. "This," our host said, "is my property. My dream is to make this land usable so we can help feed the people of this village." Before the road trip was done, our host had shown us another piece of property he had purchased near his school and told us that in that place, he had dreams to plant more crops and to maybe build a church."

When our group left for Haiti, I had told them we would be speaking in our church when we got back and that we needed to tell our brothers and sisters in Christ how God spoke to us while we were in Haiti. I wanted the people to hear how our lives had changed because of our experience. On the flight back home, this time without anyone near me who wanted to visit, it came to me why God had pushed me to go to Haiti. I thought it was because God wanted me to set a good example for my parishioners. I thought it would be a good opportunity to model what it meant to allow our faith to lead us out of our comfort zones. But now I knew why God pushed me to go to Haiti. He knew that I needed to start dreaming again. He knew that I needed a fresh infusion of hope. There were no accidents on that trip. It was not an accident that woman was placed next to me on the plane. It was no accident that our host took us to see his friends and that I had extra time to listen to their story. It was no accident that our host showed us his field and his properties. God knew that I was at a point in my life when I was living with too little hope.

It is easy to lose hope in churches in little America. While statistics show that our populations are remaining steady, the demographics of those populations are noticeably changing as many more twenty- to twenty-nine-year-olds leave little America for bigger America. I do not need statistics to tell me that. I have seen it with my very own eyes. When a young man or woman graduates from high school and heads off to college, the chances of him or her coming back to his or her hometown are slim to none. This is hard for churches. I often hear it said that "the young people are the future of our church," and while this is somewhat true, what is truer is that they are the future of someone else's church. We spend thirteen years training them up in the way they should go, and the way they go is to the places where there are more opportunities. This is not to say that little America is not being faithful and obedient in training up our next generations in the faith, but it is to say that we probably won't be the ones who receive the reward on our investment.

The moments when I have had to say goodbye to young families who have left little America to move to bigger America have been some of my hardest moments as a pastor. I have not only said goodbye to friends, but I have said goodbye to brothers and sisters in Christ who would have been pillars in the church and community if they had stayed. And I can assure you that I was not the only one grieving. When a young person or a young couple packs up and leaves little America for more opportunities somewhere, there is a great sense of sadness and grief because the whole community sees another slice of their future eaten up by the larger areas around them. When that happens, hope gets a kick in the stomach. When that happens, hope is put to the test. When that happens, hope has its elasticity tested.

But it not just the exodus of the young that leave holes in little America. The death of the elderly also leaves holes. Little America knows who their tribal leaders are. Little America knows who their matrons and patrons are. Little America cherishes and treasures the saints who have given of their time, talents, and resource for the local church and community. When one of the seasoned citizens leaves this earth, they leave a void. A speck of the salt of the earth of that community has left, and the community seems a little more bland and less appealing. How many of us in little America have not heard the stories of the "lifetimers" who played a huge role in the establishing of a trust fund or the creation of a festival or the building of a park or monument? One does not have to be in a community for long to know about the people of yesterday who are still being held on a pedestal today. And with the passing of these venerable patriarchs and matriarchs, hope gets a kick in the stomach.

Little America also gets kicked in the gut when a major employer in town either shuts down or moves to another location. In some places, when this happens, the immediate question is "I wonder who will move in to take their place?" In little America, when this happens, the immediate question is "Who will be the next to close up shop?" With the closing of a business, there is a ripple effect. Within a matter of time, the exodus begins. First, it begins as a trickle as some immediately decide that there is not any future in staying. But then the trickle morphs into a steady stream as more and more people leave. Inevitably, the effect of the closing is felt either in people resources or financial resources, but usually in both as those who stay end up taking lower-paying jobs as a sacrifice for not uprooting their families.

And the church in little America gets kicked in the gut when a staff person, even a part-time staff person, hands in his or her resignation. That person is a vital part of the operations and life of the church, and when he or she walks out the door, the church in little America wonders how or if that person will be replaced. The talent pool is small in little America as is the pool of people who are interested in coming to a small town. Speaking from experience, I know that initial reaction is "This stinks! We were just starting to get momentum with so-and-so, and now we have to start all over again, and it will probably take a while to regain that momentum."

When these things happen, hope is put to the test. When all these things happen, hope has its elasticity stretched. Maintaining hope in little America is not easy, and maybe that is why there is too often too little hope to go around in the small towns of little America.

When I think of this dearth of hope, I cannot help but think of a couple of scripture passages. The first is Isaiah 40:28: "Those who wait upon there Lord will renew their strength. They will mount up with wings like eagles. They will run and not grow weary. They will walk and not be faint." The second is from Joel 2:28: "In the last days my Spirit will come upon you and in those days the young men will dream dreams and old men will see visions."

What do these verses say to us in regard to hope? God knows how slippery hope can be and how elusive it often is. God knows that hope can very quickly slide through our fingers. God knows how easy it for us to stop dreaming. God knows how easy it is for us lament the past at the expense of longing for the future. God know that without hope we give up, that we lose all our strength, that we become chronically and spiritually fatigued.

While this is true of hope in both little and big America, I can say with confidence that little America struggles to keep hope alive. I suppose the same can be said of big America, but I have seen it over and over again in the places where I have lived. This is probably why it was so important for me to hear the dreams of the people I met on my trip to Haiti. The worst of little America is better than the best of Haiti. No one can make a strong argument that the country of Haiti can be more hopeful than the cities of little America. And it is not getting any better. The founder of Starfish has recently been sharing about the effects of COVID-19 in Haiti. Even one as optimistic and hopeful as this vibrant young man admits that the next two or three years are going to be tough. Between the virus and the elections, the country is going to need to have more people like the founder of Starfish, the lady teaching cooking, and the couple building the grocery store. These are the people who will keep Haiti afloat.

So, who will be the people who keep little America afloat? The same people: the dreamers and the hopers but not the wishful thinkers. The wishful thinkers will just keep doing things the same way, wishing for a different result. The dreamers and hopers will lean on God to give them new ideas as to how little America can thrive and not only survive. The dreamers and the hopers will believe that no matter where they live, Haiti or little America, God's plans are for his people to flourish. The dreamers and hopers will get kicked in the gut and will get back up with even more determination to go forward. The dreamers and the hopers will not be imprisoned by their situations but will rip off the chains and run to freedom.

Before I headed down to Haiti, I kept asking, "Why? Why am I going?" Maybe today those of you in little America are asking the same kind of question: "Why am I living here? Why am I not going anywhere else?" And maybe, just maybe, the answer to your question is the same answer I got: "In places where hope is in short supply, maybe I need to be the one who supplies what is needed."

4

TOO "LITTLE" COOPERATION

When my wife and I travel, we like to take the backroads of America. We like to get off the beaten path and see the America that a lot of Americans never take the time to see. Thus, we have traveled a lot of the county roads of middle and little America. When we take these roads, and even when we stay on the major thoroughfares, our eyes are not always on the road. I do not think we are much different than most people in that our eyes naturally lead us to look at things that we are interested in or are a part of our life. I think you know what I mean. If you like antiques, it is amazing how many antique stores you see on your travels. If you like farming, it is amazing how many tractors you see or how much farmland comes up to the window of your car. If you drive a convertible, you will see many more convertibles on the road than someone who does not. If you like birds, you will see more birds than anyone else. If you like to hunt, you will see deer in places that no one else ever will. Me? It is golf courses and churches, and as evidence that I still "fall short of the glory of God," I look for them in that order. When my wife is calling for an animal to come into view, I do the same ... sort of. When she is calling for a moose,

I am calling for a birdie. When I see that birdie, also known as a golf course, my mind starts asking questions of that course. I will ask, "I wonder what that course is really like. Is it easy? Is it difficult? Is it long? Is it kept in good shape? Are the greens fast? Are the fairways narrow? What would I be able to shoot if I played up to my capabilities?"

My mind does the same thing when I see churches. "I wonder what that church is really like. Would I like worshiping there? Are the people friendly? What programs do they have? What is their story? Is everyone related?" Recently, I have started asking, "Is this church winning?" Not in the sense that they are meeting their budget or growing in numbers but in the sense of "Are they making disciples?"

And then there is the other question that I ask: "Does this church do everything on their own, or are they joining forces with other churches in the area for the sake of the kingdom of God?" For a while now, it has been my belief that there are too many churches in America. When the average size of the church in America is 50 to 75, I wonder if God's church would not be more effective if instead of having three churches of fifty, there would be one church of 150. Now I am rethinking that premise and asking, "What if we kept the same amount of churches, but those churches started sharing more resources and stopped duplicating so many services? What would happen if churches started doing a better job of merging their ministries? What would happen if believers in little America started meeting together on more than Good Friday, Ash Wednesday, and other special occasions in the life of that community?"

It is my belief that we are not missing the boat in little America, but that we are leaving too much of the kingdom unbuilt because we are not working together. Through the leadership of Nehemiah, God was able to rebuild the wall of

Jerusalem in forty days. It is was an incredible feat accomplished by people working together for a common cause. So, if God can use his people to put up the walls that needed to be put up, is there any reason why God can't use his people to take down the walls that need to be taken down?

On our most recent travel through a slice of America, we came to an interesting intersection. It was not interesting because we had never seen one like it before. It grabbed my attention more because I am looking for these things now. At an intersection in rural America, there were four signs. One of them was for a church just down the road, and the other three were for three other churches, of the same denomination, also just down the road. I looked at my wife, smiled, and said, "This is what I'm talking about."

Why? Why so many churches in such a small area? What? What happened that these churches are all separate churches? When? When did this happen? Are they working together, or are they their own separate entities connected only by the steeples on the top of their buildings? And how? How are they impacting the kingdom of God? How are they doing changing people's lives? How are they doing at making a difference in the community? How are they doing at fulfilling the commission to go and make disciples who make more disciples? Forgive me, Lord, but when I saw those four signs and those four churches so close together and then the small size of the buildings, I wondered if this is really what God had in mind when he chose to build his church on us, his people. Is this the best way to win the game? Is this the best strategy to use to get us down the field? Is this a movement of the Holy Spirit or the result of past infighting and discord? Is this the result of godly men and women or tribal leaders who did not get their own way and then took their supporters and their money with them and went to play on their own field? Do you ever pause and imagine this: What could the church in little America, and big America for that matter, accomplish if we would combine our resources and all start rowing in the same direction? Can anyone argue that the simple answer is "a whole lot more"?

The loaded station wagon pulled into the only remaining campsite. Four children leaped from the vehicle and began feverishly unloading gear and setting up the tent. The boys then rushed to gather firewood, while the girls and their mother set up the camp stove and cooking utensils. A nearby camper marveled to the youngsters' father: "That, sir, is some display of teamwork."

The father replied, "I have a system. No one goes to the bathroom until the camp is set up."

If urgency is the key to teamwork, then the church should be operating with a greater sense of urgency. People have been saying this for centuries, but we know this is true: the second coming of the Lord is closer today than it has ever been. In fact, so much of biblical prophecy has been fulfilled that we can accurately say that the Lord could return at any hour. If we really care about lost souls the way we say we do and the way Jesus did, then we can no longer operate with a sense of "we've got all day."

So, why do churches not cooperate better? Why don't more churches work together? Why don't we share more resources? Why do we continue to duplicate so many services? I am going to share a list of five "cooperation crushers" that I have seen. Maybe you have not seen these, and maybe you have, but I hope this list will either start or continue the discussion either in your mind or with other people.

The first "cooperation crusher" is *theology*. To say theology is not correct. I think most churches have similar theology on the main issues of Christianity. We generally agree that God created the heavens and the earth. We generally believe that Jesus Christ is God's only begotten son and that he was conceived by the virgin Mary. We generally believe in the Holy Spirit. We generally believe that salvation is entirely by grace and not by works. We generally believe that Jesus rose from the dead and that he is the first fruits of all who believe. We generally believe in the forgiveness of sins. We generally believe that Jesus is coming again, and at that time, those who believe in him will live forever in heaven and those who do not will live forever in hell. And we generally believe that there is only one way to heaven, and that is through Jesus Christ.

The things that crush cooperation begin with the secondary issues of Christianity. When I speak of secondary issues, I am talking about things that are not essential to our salvation. I am talking about things that can and have been interpreted differently from scripture. In this category would be the sacraments, specifically Communion and baptism. Different denominations have different views on what happens with the elements in the Lord's Supper. Different denominations have different views on whether infant baptism or believer's baptism is more biblical. In this category would also be the role of the Holy Spirit and in particular the idea of a baptism of the Holy Spirit. In this category would also be the extent of sanctification. Some denominations believe that we never attain perfection on this earth but that up until the day of our death we are being sanctified. Other denominations believe that we can reach perfection on this earth. In this category would also be the distinction between Calvinism and Arminianism. There are those who believe that God's sovereignty extends to him determining everything we ever do, including whether we turn our lives to him. This is a very, very, very short definition of

Calvinism. Then there are those who believe in a much bigger role of the free will in human beings. God is sovereign, but his sovereignty is intentionally limited by God himself to give human beings greater autonomy in the decisions we make in life, including our salvation. This is a very, noticeably short definition of Arminianism. These are all significant differences, but does where we come down on these issues really impact whether we are or are not saved? I would argue that these matters are not essential to salvation.

Then we have what are probably the most prickly and contentious differences and the ones that divide us and too often keep us from cooperating—the social issues. Through the years, churches have taken different stances ranging from whether divorced people should get remarried to the right of a mother to make choices about her own body, to whether women should be in leadership positions in the church, to when civil disobedience is acceptable, to whether we should practice capital punishment, to whether members should be a part of lodges, and today, what is probably the most divisive social or biblical issue we have ever seen in our country, the views we hold on homosexuality and marriage.

Take a moment and mentally go through the list of doctrinal and social matters I have just mentioned. Are there more things that we agree on as Christians or less especially as it relates to things that are needed for salvation? Are there more things or fewer things that we could agree to disagree on with others? And then, how many dealbreakers do you see in the lists? Is there any theological, biblical, or social issue that puts up a red flag and forces you to say, "I could never cooperate with someone from a another church if they believed_____?"

And yet, how often do we fail to cooperate as churches because we believe our theology or views on matters of

Christianity are too different? Should we, then, be allowing our theology to crush our cooperation?

The second cooperation crusher is *apathy.* Let us be honest. Do most of us really care if we are working together as churches in our community? I am going to answer first here. I am guilty of this. I have never been one to come to a community and immediately seek out the pastors and find out what I can do to help them or to find out how we can help each other. The question I am now asking myself is, "Why?" Why has this never been all that important to me? Is it because this has always just been the norm wherever I have been? Is it because I think I am smarter than all the other pastors in town? Is it because I think I do not have much to offer in this area? Is it because I do not think I have the time to put in work outside the arena of the church that I am working in? Is it because I am an introvert, and I am more comfortable working by myself? Or is it because I really don't care how much impact the church is having in the community as long as the church I am serving is having an impact?

I will get into this much more later on, but I believe the reason most Christians in small communities, and probably large communities as well, don't care about working with other churches is because we only see our own churches and not God's kingdom.

I ask these questions and make this statement as a pastor, but as I look at them, I wonder if there is really any difference between the questions and comments I have made and the questions and the comments that a vast majority of church attenders in little America would make? I think not. I have had a number of people come into my office through the years, and they have brought up a number of different matters, but I have never had someone come into my office and say, "Pastor,

I really want us to find a way to cooperate more with the other churches in town. What can I do?" Likewise, I have sat in on many church board meetings and rare has been the time when the church leaders asked each other, "What are we doing to cooperate with the other churches in town and what can we do as a board to do that?

Oh, it happens through the year when the community is having a special celebration, the community has encountered a special need, or the community has a tradition of gathering for a special holiday, but in the natural course of normal day-to-day living in a community, how much and how often do we really think about what could happen if we would join forces with the other churches in town?

And why is that? We really do not care, do we?

The third cooperation crusher is *independence* or, in other words, "I can do it myself." We come by this attitude very naturally and at a young age. If you don't remember saying it yourself, you most certainly remember a time when one of your children or grandchildren made this bold proclamation. The message comes through loud and clear: "I am more than capable of handling this without any help." While we may find this statement of independence somewhat amusing coming from the mouth of a youngster, the humor of it fades proportionately to the age of the person saying it. How many of us haven't been frustrated with our parents as they age and we want to return the help they once gave to us only to be rebuffed in our effort of kindness and assistance?

Churches in little America do not verbalize this statement of independence, but our actions speak very loudly. Although almost every church struggles and almost every church has areas where they are deficient, how often do we ever go to another church and ask, "Could you help us? We would like to do this, but we realize that as much as we would like, we can't do it by ourselves?"

So why don't we ask for help? Why are churches so bound and determined that we are going to do things by ourselves? I will throw out a few reasons for you to chew on. One reason might be that it is too much work to work with others. We like doing things by ourselves because it is easier. We know how we do things. We know the standards we have set. We know where everything is at. We trust ourselves more than we trust others.

Another reason might be that it takes too much time to do things with others. When we work with others, we must work with or around multiple schedules rather than just one. Doing things by ourselves takes phone calls and texts and waiting for responses out of the equation. We balance the plusses and minuses of doing something with someone else, and we determine that it is more efficient to go it alone.

Another reason is pride. We are a people who do not like to ask for help. Like Peter in the upper room, it is much easier for us accept the role of washing the feet of others than it is to accept the role of having our feet washed by someone else. If you have ever been in both positions—foot-washer and foot-washee—you know what I am talking about. Our pride makes us more comfortable being the helper than the helpee. Our pride keeps us from being comfortable being dependent on others. Our pride keeps us from admitting our shortcomings.

A final reason I set before you is that people in little America are just used to working alone. I know this is probably too broad of a generality, but, proportionately, more people in little America either work by themselves or with a small number of others. The agricultural economy is often a driving force in little America, and who figures most prominently in that economy? The farmers. Whom do farmers usually work with?

Themselves and maybe another family member or two or three. Small businesses are prominent in little America. Go down Main Street, and what do you see? Mom-and-pop stores on both sides of the street and insurance agencies with the last names of the agents on the signs or on the window. In communities of less than four thousand, unless they are in a tourist area, you do not see many chain stores. In communities of less than four thousand, you don't see a lot of businesses that employ over one hundred people. The result is that most people in little America are used to working either alone or with only a few other people. Thus, the natural reaction when it comes to working together as churches is to lean into doing what we are accustomed to doing, which is "doing it by ourselves."

The fourth cooperation crusher is *competition*. Unfortunately, churches are like most entities in that over time we become territorial. This makes sense because whom are churches composed of? Sinners. As such, we are composed of the same type of people that all other entities are composed of. However, this is not to excuse this behavior. Given the truth that we are sinners, why is it that churches can be so competitive? One of the reasons was mentioned in the chapter on too little hope. The pool of people to draw from in little America is not that large. The largest pool is those who used to be in church but for a variety of reasons are no longer interested. These are difficult fish to catch. Before bringing them in, they need to be broken down. The formerly churched have a lot of "church" baggage that pushes them as far away from the doorway of a church as possible. Many of them have had a bad experience with the church. Many of them are battling mental images of the church being irrelevant, impersonal, and unimportant. Many of them still see themselves as good people and good citizens and thus as not needing the dynamics of the church in their life.

If we are going to be unable to reach the formerly churched in the traditional ways many churches are committed to, then whom are they are going to reach? The Welcome Wagon went out of business many years ago in your town because so few people were moving in, and those who did move in more than likely had family in the area so the church they checked out was the one where their parents or aunts and uncles or cousins or siblings attended. So that shrinks the pool even more.

The pool shrinks even further when we take out the unbelievers in town. While this group should be our target audience, we have a tendency to shy away from this group in little America. Remember, little America is guilty of stereotyping, and thus the people in this group have often been pegged as untouchable or unreachable because we see them for who they have been rather than who they can be. On the chance we would reach them, would we really want to keep them? Investing in the unbelievers is a messy job. They likely have issues in their life that make them high maintenance. They could have substance abuse issues or marriage issues or sexual issues or legal issues, and because the church in little America doesn't have a lot of experience in addressing these issues, the "dirt" in these lives makes us apprehensive and scared.

So, whom then does that leave? People who are already in the other churches. It is the sheep in the pastures of the other churches who are our targets. We would never admit that we would want another church in town to close or to have problems that might drive some of their members away, but you don't have to stick your ear too close to the pavement to hear, "Do you think we will get so and so if their church closes or their pastor leaves or the little squabble in their church escalates into something bigger?" What happens when we entertain such a line of thinking? Competition. We see our church declining, and we are start thinking about how we are going to survive so we set our sights on the targets we will be most comfortable having around if we snag them. If we are honest, the desired targets for attendance in churches in little America are the people who are already worshiping in another one of the churches in town.

Finally, competition comes about because of bad blood between a couple of churches in town. We like to think of little America as the idyllic place that is depicted by poets, writers, and songwriters—you know, the place where everyone gets along and the people will live happily ever after or until the Lord returns. This is not the case. Just because people live together in close quarters in little America does not mean that they love their neighbor. The aftershocks of a disagreement can last for generations. The Hatfields and the McCoys are not fictional characters. The repercussions of a split decision can reverberate through all the halls of a village, including the halls of God's house. When we see a few churches of the same denomination in a small town, it behooves us to do a little digging into the why of this occurrence. It may take some time, and you won't usually get the real story the first few times you ask, but behind the signs in the front of the building, there are probably some hard feelings still percolating inside the building. Because of these hard feelings, these churches will not be rooting for the success of their sister church or daughter church or illegitimate child church.

In the Hebrew language, the root for the words *curse* and *bless* are the same. This means that something can be both a blessing and curse at the same time. It is this way with the spirit of competition. Being competitive can be a good thing. Being competitive keeps us from complacency. Being competitive pushes us to be better. Being competitive brings enjoyment to an activity. But being competitive can also be a bad thing. Being competitive is a bad thing when both parties should be striving for the same results. Being competitive is a bad thing when it affects our sportsmanship. Being competitive is a bad thing when it divides us rather than unites us. Being competitive is a bad thing when it keeps churches from cooperating in the mission to build the kingdom of God.

I have the privilege of coaching our town's high school golf team. This past year, I had the special privilege of coaching a team that went to the state tournament for the first time in thirty-seven years and only the second time in school history. There were obviously a few things that brought great joy and pleasure to the season, but there is one thing in particular that stands out. Our team of fifteen was pretty much divided between five good players and ten not-so-good players. The beauty of this team, though, is that it was not two teams but one. I have never had a team where the poorer players were more willing to ask the better players for help and, what was even cooler, where the better players were quick to come alongside the poorer players and help them out. It was truly a team of kids who cooperated with each other. They were competitive with each other—not in a way that divided them but that brought out the best in them. I believe from the bottom of my heart that not only did this contribute to our appearance at state but that the memories of this spirit of cooperation will last with these kids for years to come.

What is true on a sports team should be the same with churches. Cooperation should be important to us. Would anyone argue that God wants all the churches in a town to do things on their own? Would anyone argue that God is pleased when we all go our own way and do our own thing? Would anyone argue that the church can do more when we pool our resources and stop duplicating our services? Would anyone argue that the church in little America can improve when it comes to cooperating more with each other?

5

TOO "LITTLE" FOCUS

I finished the last chapter referring to my privilege of being the golf coach at our local high school. When I begin a season, I always meet with the kids and their parents, and I always tell them that I am not really a golf coach. The upperclassmen then usually give a hearty "You said it, Coach!" before I can explain myself. As I continue, I tell them that I am really a life coach who happens to use golf to teach life lessons. Here is an example of one of those lessons. During a practice round, I will continually tell kids that the most important thing they do when hitting a shot is what they do before they do anything. For some reason, I get kids who think they need to take twenty-five practice swings before they hit their actual shot. Very quickly I tell them that two practice swings are more than adequate. Because they are young and still flexible, rigor mortis is not going to set in between shots so they can save their energy for the real thing. Instead of taking practice swings, I encourage the kids to stand behind the ball, decide on a target, visualize the shot, and then address the ball, and hit it.

Now why do I advocate and preach this as the best thing they can do before they ever start their swing? Because for any

shot in golf to be good, we need to know what our target is. If
we choose the wrong target, even if we hit the ball correctly, the
results will be bad unless by the grace of God you hit the shot
wrong and you accidently send it toward the right target. I will
never get on kids if they choose the right target and then have
a mishit. But if they choose the wrong target, then we will have
a conversation. This goes for every shot the kid hits on a hole.

When you stand on the tee box and look toward the green,
there will be lot of targets to look at, of which several may be
okay to shoot at. The key is to pick out the best target. When
you stand in the fairway, or too often the rough with my kids,
there will once again be any number of targets to pick from. The
key is to pick the best target … maybe a tree behind the green,
maybe the edge of a bunker in front of the green, and maybe a
side of the green away from the hole. The goal is to get your next
shot not just to an okay place but to the best place possible. And
then once on the green, the exercise is repeated once again. If
it is a downhill putt, the target may be two feet in front of the
hole. If it is putt that will break quite a bit, it may be two feet
to the side of the hole. If it is an uphill putt, it may be two feet
behind the hole. The truth is that the best target may not always
be the hole itself even though the goal is to get the ball into the
hole in the least number of strokes possible.

Here is the lesson for the church. When we look out from
our church buildings, there will be a lot of different targets we
can pick from. Many of them will not be bad choices. The key
is to find the best target and then commit to aiming for that
target. Unless we have identified the best target, even our best
efforts will not bring about the desired result. Sometimes, by
the grace of God, we will accidentally hit the best target, but
poor aim generally equates to poor results. One of the reasons
the church in little America, and the church in general, is not

having the impact we would want and isn't getting the results we want is that we have either chosen the wrong target or haven't really even chosen a target.

If you ask most churchgoers in little America what they are aiming at, or what their focus is, you will more than likely get a blank stare or a generic religious answer. Like the kids on my golf team who want to take a bunch of practice swings but don't see the need to pick a target, too many churches are busy doing their practice swings, or their church activities, without ever knowing exactly what they are trying to hit. In this chapter, I want to focus on just a couple of the targets that can be attractive for churches to aim at but targets, nonetheless, that are not targets that, even if they are hit, will propel the church to have the impact on their people, their community, and, most important, the kingdom of God that God desires and has designed for his church.

The targets I am directing your focus on are not unique to little America but are certainly prevalent in little America. Obviously, there are more than a couple of targets that churches focus on. In truth, the number of targets that churches focus on can be the basis for entire books and include such targets as social justice, feeding the poor, domestic and foreign missions, and attracting seekers. All of these are noble targets, but the question must always be "Are they the best targets?" If we hit these targets, will we really achieve our goal? If we hit these targets, will we be accomplishing all that God desires and has designed for his church?

The first target that little America spends a lot of time focusing on is *feel-good moments*. Back when I was growing up, there was a song that became quite popular in church circles. The song was "Kumbaya," which translated into English is "Come by Here." The origins of this song have been enveloped in mystery for nearly a century. Some have said that it came from Africa. Others have claimed authorship and even copyrighted it. Some grew up singing it around campfires at summer camp accompanied by folk guitar and three chords. It has been sung at protest marches and candlelight vigils. Those who came of age during the 1960s and 1970s during the Vietnam War heard Joan Baez (b. 1941) and Pete Seeger (1919–2014) sing this song, as well as Odetta (1930–2008) and the all-women African American a cappella ensemble Sweet Honey in the Rock. Indeed, "Kumbaya" was a significant Civil Rights song sung by protestors.

The backlash associated with the song during the last three decades is a curious turn of events. Song critic, Stephen Winick summarizes this well:

> Politically, ["Kumbaya"] became shorthand for weak consensus seeking that fails to accomplish crucial goals. Socially, it came to stand for the touchy-feely, the wishy-washy, the nerdy, and the meek. These recent attitudes toward the song are unfortunate, since the original is a beautiful example of traditional music, dialect, and creativity. However, the song's recent fall from grace has at least added some colorful metaphors to American political discourse, such phrases as "to join hands and sing "Kumbaya," which means to ignore our differences and get along (albeit superficially), and "Kumbaya moment," an event at which such naïve bonding occurs.

The history of the song leads us along a weaving, winding road that traveled today, no longer is getting us to the most important place we can be as a church. We all long for "good feeling" moments, and I am no exception. I love those times when I feel a glow coming over my face, peace coming into my heart, and a lightness of step emanating from my feet. Add in a few goosebumps, and the elements combine to leave me echoing the words of Peter when he was on the Mount of Transfiguration: "Can't I just stay here for a while?"

The problem, as the story of "Kumbaya" illustrates, is that the yearning for feel-good moments often keeps us from really dealing with the real issues of life and, in the context of this book, the real issues of the kingdom of God. In our desire to avoid conflict, in our desire to ignore that which is ugly, in our longing to just get along, we too often sacrifice what is most important for what is most pleasant.

The church in little America has too often shoved important matters under the rug for the sake of getting along. The problem with shoving things under the rug is that we can only ignore these things for so long until they make their way out from underneath the rug and, like garbage that isn't disposed of, have a smell that has just gotten worse with age and neglect. We can only sing "Kumbaya" around the campfire for so long until the fire of the moment burns out, and we must take care of the ashes and embers.

So why does the church in little America focus so much on "Kumbaya" moments even to the detriment of the kingdom of God? It can be that we all know each other so well. We are afraid of confronting difficult issues or people because we know that others know what is in our closets and the risk of that being exposed is not worth the confrontation. It can be that we have been burned by saying something not realizing that the person at the center of a problem was related to three-quarters of the people in the church and half the people in town. The pain of having our words or actions coming back at us is often too much for us to bear. It can be that we just do not know how to have difficult conversations or how to navigate through difficult moments, and thus we take the easy route and avoid everything. It can be that we just do not think that addressing the elephant in the room is worth it. Even if the elephant is addressed, not much is going to change, so why take the time and make the effort to deal with it.

The net result is that we get along on the surface, we have our momentary feel-good moments, and we make our way our through the waters of life without capsizing, but we don't really accomplish all that much for the kingdom. "Kumbaya" moments are not bad. In fact, they are enjoyable, and they are pleasant respites from the drudgery of life, but are "feel-good moments" the best target for the church to aim at? Is this where our focus is to be? When Jesus gave his final address to his disciples, I don't remember him telling us to go out into the world and provide feel-good moments for the world. Do you remember any of that?

The second target that churches in little America often choose is *caring for each other.* Now, once again, caring for each other is a good target. The Bible is full of verses telling us to love each other, care for each other, and come alongside each other. The Bible tells us that we need to be taking care of our widows and widowers. The Bible tells us we need to be taking care of the poor. The Bible tells us we need to give honor to our mothers and fathers and others who are part of the generation ahead of us. The Bible tells us that we need to rejoice with those who are rejoicing and to weep with those who are weeping. The Bible tells us that we to be there to help carry the burdens of others. The Bible tells us we need to visit those in nursing homes. (There is no specific verse for this, but the message is clear.)

So why is caring for others not the best place for us to put our focus? Why is caring for others not the best target for us to aim at? What happens is that caring for others too often becomes confined to taking care of our own. If you have ever been a part of a prayer meeting in little America or been present at a worship service where prayer requests are taken from the congregation, you know that almost all of the time, the prayer requests are for the physical health of people in either our biological or church family. This is not bad. It is good for us to pray for the hip of an aunt or the upcoming thyroid surgery for one of our brothers or for the loss of a job for one of our children. This is all good. This is all needed. This is all biblical.

But how often do we hear someone say, "Will you please pray for my neighbor? He doesn't know the Lord, and I can't find a way to connect with him?" or "Will you please pray for my niece. She is making really bad choices in her life that are pulling her away from the Lord," or "Will you please pray for the inmates in our county jail? They are in bondage to so many bad things, and they need spiritual freedom from that bondage."

I think you know what I am talking about. This doesn't happen all the time, but it happens too often, and the things we pray about are usually the things that matter the most to us.

This same idea carries over to the people we will go see. The church in little America is great at going to see aged relatives. The church in little America is great at making hospital visits. The church in little America is great at reaching out to people who have gone through a calamity. The church in little America is great at coming alongside someone who needs help with a project. It is this this care and these acts of kindness that often make little America such a special place to live. It is one of the things that make living in little America pleasurable to me. I know that when I am going through a tough time, there will be people who will be there for me.

But with all the positives and the Biblical backing for focusing on caring for others, is this the best target for us to be aiming at? For all the benefits that come from being there for others, is this where our primary attention needs to be? When Jesus gave his final pep talk to his disciples, did he tell them to go out into the world and care for each other? Oh, this was a ramification of what he told them. This would be a by-product of what he told them. But was caring for each other the Great Commission he left them with? Do not mistake what I am getting at here. I am not saying that we should not be caring for each other. We should. The needs of others is a good place to put our focus. But is caring for each other the best and most important target we are to be focusing on?

The final target that I see the church in little America giving too much attention to is *Biblical education*. Once again, do not shoot me. I know what the Bible says about knowing the word. I know that a whole long psalm was written on the importance of knowing the ways and precepts and statutes of the Lord. It is too bad that Psalm 119 gets a bad rap because of its length. It is really a beautiful exposé on the value of knowing the Word of God. I know that God said in Hosea 4:6 (NIV) "that we perish for lack of knowledge." I know that Paul spent the first parts of his letters, especially his letter to the Ephesians, teaching and reminding the members of the churches of what they were to believe concerning Jesus Christ and all the matters pertaining to salvation through him.

The problem that comes when we make attaining Biblical knowledge our main focus is that too often we make the acquisition of that knowledge more important than the application of that knowledge. It is great when God's people get together to study the Bible. It is not as great when those people learn the Word and then are not transformed by the Word. James says it so well in James 1:22 (NIV): "Do not merely listen to the word, and so deceive yourselves. Do what it says." It is great when God's people get together to study the Bible. It is not as great when that group becomes stagnant and the effects of that study do not have any ripple effects on others or the community. It is great when God's people get together to study the Bible. It is not so great when it comes to application of the passage, and they use the pronouns "they" and "them" and not "I." It is great when God's people get together to study the Bible. It is not so great when we do not then take someone who is unfamiliar with God's word under our wings and walk with that person through the scriptures.

I haven't taken the time to do a survey to find out for sure if churchgoers in little America know their Bibles considerably better than churchgoers in bigger America, but I can almost guarantee that they do. So if that is the case—and I believe it is, and I believe you believe it is as well—then why isn't little America the healthiest and most robust segment of society as it relates to impact-making churches? Or if it is healthier than the church in bigger America, why is it not showing up better? Why are the formerly churched still the largest segment of the population in little America? If Biblical knowledge is the best target for us to shoot for and if we are hitting the target consistently, then why isn't the church in little America reaching more unbelievers?

Once again, I ask the question, "When Jesus gave his final address to his disciples when he left them did he tell them to make biblical education the top priority, or was it something else?" I know that part of his Great Commission was to teach people all that he had commanded them, but if Biblical knowledge was the very, very best target, then why wasn't biblical knowledge emphasized in his first words? I am not a Greek scholar, but I do know that in the Greek language, correct grammar is not as important as getting the most important aspect of a truth at the beginning of the sentence.

The problem with churches in little America is not that we are not focusing on good targets … We are. Making times when we feel good is a good target. Caring for each other is a good target. Gaining Biblical knowledge is a good target. The problem is that we are not focusing and putting our attention and effort at hitting the best target, which is, as you can tell from my references to Jesus's final pep talk to his disciples, making disciples. The targets we are aiming at are not bad targets; it is just that the effects of hitting these things should either be the means to help us hit the best target or the by-products of hitting the best target. These targets should not be our first priorities.

Hebrews 12:1–3 gives us further insight into this matter. The writer to the Hebrews tells us in these verses that we need to throw off everything that encumbers us and the sin that so easily entangles us. That which encumbers and the sin that entangles are two different categories of things. The sin that entangles us is clearly the bad things in life that can be our focus and priority. The things that encumber, though, are the things in life that are good but are not the best for us if we are going to win a race. While these words were written to individuals, the truth is the same for the church. If we are going to win, there are some good things we take off or lay aside.

God knows that laying these good things aside is not easy for us, so he gives us direction as to how we can go about doing that. This is where singleness of focus comes in. God's word tells us that we need to fix our eyes on Jesus.

In the ancient Greco-Roman world, running was one of

the most popular of the Olympic games. The place prepared for the race was called the stadium because its length equaled a stadion, or six hundred Greek feet. The stadium was an oblong area, with a straight wall across one end, where the entrances were, the other end being round and entirely closed. Tiers of seats were on either side for the spectators. The starting place was at the entrance end and was marked by a square pillar. At the opposite end was the goal, where the judge sat and held the prize. The eyes of the competitors remained fixed on him. This picture is being painted with the phrase "fix your eyes on Jesus."

The Greek word for "fixing" is a much fuller word than we can find in the English language. It has a preposition in it that turns the look away from everything else or to look from all else to Jesus. Do not fix your gaze on the cloud of witnesses; they will hinder you if they take away your eye from Jesus. Do not look at the weights and the besetting sin—these you have laid aside; look away from them. Do not even look at the racecourse, or the competitors, but look to Jesus. The instructive original has in it the word "eis," which is translated "on," but in addition has the force of "into." We will do well if we look on Jesus, but better still if we are found "looking into Jesus."

This is not only good advice for us as individuals to help us navigate through life, but it is also good advice for us as churches if we are to navigate through the challenges of the twenty-first century. If the church in little America is going to win again, we must focus into the most important target for the church to aim at: the target of making disciples who make disciples.

Roger Bannister became the first man in history to run a mile in less than four minutes. Within two months, John Landy eclipsed the record by 1.4 seconds. On August 7, 1954, the two met together for a historic race. As they moved into the last lap, Landy held the lead. It looked as if he would win, but as he neared the finish, he was haunted by the question, "Where is Bannister?" As he turned to look, Bannister took the lead. Landy later told a *Time* magazine reporter, "If I hadn't looked back, I would have won!"

The lesson for the church? If we are going to look around at targets that are less than the best, it is going to hinder our chances of winning the race. The only way for the church in little America to start winning again is to stop focusing on targets that are simply good and commit to focusing on the target that is the best.

6

NET RESULT: TOO "LITTLE" IMPACT

So, what is the net result of too little of too much? What is the effect of too little repentance? What is the effect of too little of a God? What is the effect of too little hope? What is the effect of too little cooperation? What is the effect of too little focus? The net result is that the churches in little America are not having the impact on either their communities or the kingdom of God and vice versa. But do not take my word for it. I will warn you in advance that unless you like statistics and data, you are going to find this chapter to be somewhat dry. If you do like statistics and data, you still may find this chapter to be somewhat dry. My aim here is not to use specific statistics to convince you that the church in little America is not having the impact it should but rather to paint a larger picture with statistics to make this point. To do this, I am pulling out paintbrushes from Gallup, Barna, and the Pew Research Center, as well as some additional brushes from some other studies I found while perusing the internet. While I don't claim to have any real artistic talent, I do believe that putting together this smorgasbord of data will help you get a clear picture of what is, and is not, happening in the little America in regard to the church.

In a Gallup article written by Jeffrey Jones and published in a Chegg Study periodical research shows that US church membership was 70 percent or higher from 1937 through 1976 before falling modestly to an average of 68 percent in the 1970s through the 1990s. The past twenty years have seen an acceleration in the drop-off, with a twenty-percentage-point decline since 1999.

In 2019, the Pew Research Center published an article entitled, "In U.S., Decline of Christianity Continues at a Rapid Pace." The first paragraph of the article summarizes their findings this way:

> The religious landscape of the United States continues to change at a rapid clip. In Pew Research Center telephone surveys conducted in 2018 and 2019, 65% of American adults describe themselves as Christians when asked about their religion, down 12 percentage points over the past decade. Meanwhile, the religiously unaffiliated share of the population, consisting of people who describe their religious identity as atheist, agnostic or "nothing in particular," now stands at 26%, up from 17% in 2009.

An article written by Aaron Earls for Lifeway Research has information that I find to be relevant to little America in that little America is dotted with more mainline denomination churches than bigger America. According to research done by Earl, attendance in nonmainline churches has remained steady for the past twenty years, while attendance in mainline churches has dropped by 20 percent from 39 percent to 10 percent.

One can draw a lot of conclusions from statistics, and not

all of them are accurate, but based on the disparity in numbers between those churches labeled as "evangelical" and those labeled as "mainline denomination," it certainly seems to me that mainline denomination churches have not been as strong at getting into the community and staying in touch with people as they should be. And the numbers are proving it.

An interesting sidebar to this data is a finding of the Barna group concerning women and church attendance. For years, the gap between the percentage of women who attend church and that of men who attended was significant with the women being the far larger percentage. That is now changing, according to the Barna group.

According to Barna's research, among practicing Christians in the Households of Faith report, mothers are more likely to provide encouragement, advice, and sympathy to their teenagers than fathers. Teenagers are also more likely to seek out their mothers more often than their fathers to discuss faith, the Bible, and things that bother them. On a variety of dimensions of activity, these Christian women appear to be more present in the lives of their children than men.

Beyond the household, how are women present as part of a church family? Writing for the Barna Group, Dr. Ryan Burge writes,

> The data from the last sixteen years tells an interesting story. Women were consistently more likely than men to attend church weekly in the 2000's. However, two important trends have emerged since 2012. The first is that attendance has declined significantly for both men and women. However, the rate of decline for female respondents is much more dramatic.

> In 2009, 48 percent of women attended church at least once a week, but, in less than a decade, the share has dropped to 31 percent. The data indicate that women are no more likely to be actively churched in 2020 than men."

The numbers are clear that the church in general, and by extension, the church in little America, is losing ground. With each ensuing generation, the percentage of people who are interested and active in the church continues to decline. But because numbers can be twisted and skewed and can fail to take into consideration all the factors involved in a given situation or scenario, we need to take out a brush and fill in the spots on the canvas that the numbers fail to address..

The brushes I went to were studies on social issues and the comparisons between urban and rural, or big and little, America. I wanted to see if the church in little America was indeed making a difference even though the numbers said otherwise. I will let you draw your own conclusions.

I looked for the divorce rates in urban and rural America. In this case rural, or little, America was doing much better. While the study is on the older side, ten years to be exact, the article entitled "Economics of the World" noted that around the world, the proportion of people getting divorced in urban areas is 25 percent higher than in rural areas, the country being the same.

This is the positive news. The rest of the studies I found are not so good. In a *Time* article from March 9, 2015, Justin Worland reports that "young people who live in rural areas kill themselves at twice the rate as youth who live in cities, according to a new study in the journal JAMA Pediatrics."

What about substance abuse? Writing for the Addiction

Center, Natalie Hoeg shares the following: "Researchers have discovered that those who reside in rural areas not only abused drugs more frequently, but they also began doing so at a much younger age than those in urban areas."

The Addiction Center also did a study on alcohol use in rural and urban America in 2006 and found that "alcohol abuse exceeded illicit drug abuse in rural areas, and that it has been particularly prevalent among rural youth."

So where is the church in all of this? If the church in little America was really making an impact on their communities and the kingdom of God, would we still be seeing these numbers and these trends?

Neglect and abuse of children is also present in rural communities. A 2010 report to Congress from the Administration for Children and Families (ACF) states that the reported incidence for all categories of maltreatment except educational neglect was higher in rural counties than in urban counties, with rural children being almost twice as likely to experience maltreatment, including overall abuse, sexual abuse, emotional abuse, and neglect.

What about the rate of teen pregnancies? A report on Iowa PBS in 2016 noted that fewer teens are giving birth nationwide, but new government data reveal that teen births are much higher in rural areas than urban ones.

In urban counties with large populations, 18.9 teens per 1,000 females age fifteen to nineteen gave birth in 2015, far lower than in rural counties with populations of fewer than 50,000 people, which reported a significantly higher teen birth rate (30.9), according to a new report from the National Center for Health Statistics.

And sexually transmitted diseases (STDs)? A report in the

Journalist's Resource written by Chloe Reichel in 2019 reported that

> sexually transmitted infection rates for chlamydia, gonorrhea and syphilis are at all-time highs, according to the U.S. Centers for Disease Control and Prevention's Sexually Transmitted Disease Surveillance Report. Between 2016 and 2017, rates of chlamydia increased by 6.9%, totaling 1.7 million reported cases. Gonorrhea rates increased 18.6% over the same one-year period, with 555,608 cases reported in 2017. And 30,664 cases of syphilis were reported in 2017, increasing by 10.5% over a one-year period.

The article continues by saying that new research suggests that the spread of these infections is particularly affecting rural areas, where these diseases had been less common. Historically, STDs had been concentrated mostly in urban areas.

Where is the church in little America in all of this? When our eyeballs tell us that there are more churches and more churchgoers per person in rural areas, then why are so many of our social ills worse in little America? Researchers have given a number of scientific and sociological and psychological reasons, and these are valid reasons, but if the church in little America was really making the impact that it should and that we want to think it is, then these statistics and these data would not be nearly so discouraging. Where is the church in all of this?

I think I have an idea. Over six years ago, I moved to my present call. A little over a month into my call, the three churches of my denomination that are within twelve miles of each other started a venture that would come to be called Thrive Ministries. The purpose of this venture was to breathe life into our three churches. Two of the churches were in decline and had been so for several years. The church I pastor knew that unless they took some transformational steps, they would be in that place soon. The result of a year of discussions and conversations was Thrive Ministries. The goal of Thrive Ministries was to help all three churches, or campuses, become better at making disciples. The way to do that was to combine resources and stop duplicating services while at the same time keeping all the church doors open. To make a long story short, a couple of months ago, the plug was pulled on this venture. It was not an easy decision. Many of the leadership team of Thrive felt that we had made a lot of progress and that Thrive was making a big impact. A member from one of the campuses made the comment that his or her church had never been healthier.

That being so, I was not a very popular person when I raised these two questions: "How many adult baptisms have our churches had in the past five years?" and "How many unchurched people are now visiting our churches because of relationships we have built with them?" Everyone in the room knew that the answer to both questions was zero. And yet, that being the case, the leadership team could not and would not admit that Thrive Ministries was not working.

I share this story not to disparage the leadership team of Thrive Ministries because I do not think they are any different than most church members in little America. We are good people. We will not be the people on TV looting buildings. We will not be the people with our names in the newspaper for various indiscretions. We will not be the people who will drive other people out of our towns. But just because we are good people does not mean we are people of impact in the kingdom of God.

As we come closer and closer to the return of Christ, zero adult baptisms in five years is not going to cut it. As the world around us and the walls within our little communities break apart at a faster rate, kumbaya moments are not going to cut it. As the world is filled with more and more hurting people, just caring for our own is not going to cut it. We must start walking across our lawns and our streets and into the lives of our neighbors. As more and more people want a cause to support, having head knowledge of the Bible is not going to cut it. The world will need to see the practical outcome of what we have learned. As each successive generation becomes more and more unchurched, opening our doors and hoping others come through them is not going to cut it. Gone are the days of waiting for others to come to us. We must be going to them, which was the original message from Jesus all along. The church in little America needs to start making a bigger impact on our communities and on the kingdom of God. We did it before, and we can do it again.

And there is hope. We can win again. We can change the trajectory of our future. We can prove the prognosticators wrong. We can be the inspiration for an entire nation. The next section of the book will spell out how that can happen. Just a little spoiler alert: we do not have to reinvent the wheel.

A "LITTLE" STRATEGY

1

GO FOR THE GOAL LINE ... NOT THE FIFTY-YARD LINE

When I was growing up, there was one week during the summer that was better than all the rest. It was not the week of our family vacation. It was not the first week out of school. It was not the week that Little League baseball started. It was the week of vacation Bible school (VBS). This was my favorite week of the summer. Our church used a ministry called Rural Bible Mission. An "uncle" would come every year and lead us in singing, crafts, Bible stories, and snacks. But the part of the week that I enjoyed the most was the punch cards. Part of the Rural Bible Mission program was giving punch cards to everyone who came. What was the beauty and joy of the punch cards? There was a weeklong competition to see who could get the most punches. *I loved the competition!* How did you earn punches on your card? One of the ways was by winning a chorus drill. The piano player would play a note or two or more, and the first person to guess the song got a punch. Another way to earn a punch was to win a Bible drill. Oh, how I remember those powerful words. As the words "Gentlemen, start your engines" was a national treasure for so many years at the Indianapolis 500, the words, "Everyone, Bibles up, draw swords, charge," were a local treasure I looked forward to hearing every year. I can still hear the pages of the Bibles being ruffled through as we raced to find that Bible verse that would earn us a coveted punch. Not to brag, but I won a good share of those Bible drills and won and a good number of punches in those competitions. But the most punches were earned by memorizing scripture. On the bottom third of the card were several Bible verses and passages to learn during the week, and for every verse we memorized, we got a hole punched in our card. I still look back on those weeks as the time when I learned my Bible more than any other time.

Because I had such pleasant memories of VBS and because I experienced the great impact of learning the books of the Bible and memorizing scripture, I have tried to incorporate some of that into my years of ministry. Unfortunately, the results have not been what I have hoped for. One of the reasons is that very few kids are as competitive as I was, but the bigger reason is the pushback I got from parents and church leaders. The reason for the pushback? "It's not healthy to have this kind of competition because those who don't win or those who don't wish to join in end up feeling left out and degraded."

It is probably best that I do not say anything more about our culture of participation ribbons except to say that I see this mentality of minimizing winning and rewarding simple participation impacting the effectiveness of the church in a negative way. The church today, and particularly what I have seen in little America, has made getting in the game the goal rather than winning the game. We have too many churches where the goal is getting more people to win varsity letters and fewer people to score touchdowns.

Let us use a football analogy to flush this out. Now, I love watching football, but playing football was never in the cards for me. Remember, I am an expert on little, and little and football do not go together. I was unfortunate enough to be dealt the triumvirate of physical qualities of little, slow, and weak and thus was destined at an early age to be the statistician and not the quarterback. Still, this is what I have seen.

The church in little America, and probably big America as well, has made the goal to get people into the game even if that means spending their entire time at the fifty-yard line. Now the fifty-yard line has a place in the game. It is midfield, after all. It is a rather neutral place. Not a lot usually happens at the fifty-yard line except for changes of possessions. Every once in a while, a big play happens, but for a majority of the game, not much scoring takes place when players are at the fifty-yard line. A game played at the fifty-yard line usually ends up as a 0–0 tie, but at the end of the game, there are still high fives and affirmations from the coaches about the effort put forth and energy expended. But, as is said about ties, they are as rewarding as kissing your cousin. If a football coach would say that his goal is get to the fifty-yard line, and that was it, we would look at the coach and encourage him to find another job. He may rebut, "But I got a lot of players in the game, and we had a bigger team than our opponents."

Silly, isn't it? And yet I believe this has become the mind-set in the church in little America. Because the numbers in little America are dwindling, our goal has changed from winning the game to just having a team, and if we win, that is just icing on the cake. The result is that our churches are giving out participation ribbons to everyone who enters their doors, and those who join the family of God are content to just get to heaven. In effect then, we have a church culture where the fifty-yard line is not only the middle of the field but also the end zone.

There are some churches, however, that are not content to scrimmage at midfield. Some know that they need to get down the field. That being the case, churches develop youth programs, seniors' programs, attractive worship services, a small group here and there, and a token ministry in the community. There is nothing wrong with this. These are good developments, but to continue with the football analogy, these efforts, or plays, help get the church further down the field and into field-goal range. The quality of the programs and the quality of the worship service and the quality of the sermon help the church put points on the board. A field goal is better than no points at all, but how many teams win a game just by kicking field goals? Four field goals is twelve points. How many times is twelve points enough to win the game? Still, we celebrate field goals. We high-five ourselves, and we celebrate that what we are doing is keeping us in the game. We return to the same plays that helped us get down to the thirty- or twenty-yard line, and overall, we feel pretty good about ourselves. We have kept having a team, and we have a few good things going with the team. And every once in a while, we are the recipients of a divine accident or a hail Mary, and we cross the goal line, which is a reason for lengthy celebration and for recording in the oral history of the church to use as a point of reference and rebuttal whenever anyone has the gall to say that our team isn't that good, and there is plenty of room for improvement.

The better teams are the teams that make it into the red zone on a regular basis. Praise the Lord for the churches that are making progress. Praise the Lord for the churches that are using their personnel wisely. Praise the Lord for the churches that are using innovative strategies to advance the ball. Praise the Lord for the churches that know what they do well and then practice those tasks repeatedly, fine-tuning their plays in a manner such that the details and nuances are accounted for. Praise the Lord for churches that have a heart and a beating pulse for the people in their community who are not in the game or on the team but would be interested if they were approached and cared for. Praise the Lord for churches for whom the one lost sheep is as important as the ninety-nine that are already in the fold.

Still, ask any coach or offensive player where the toughest twenty yards are on the football field, and they will tell you the twenty yards closest to their opponent's goal line. Likewise, ask any coach or defensive player what part of the field they have to defend with the greatest intensity and effort, and they will tell you the twenty yards closest to their own goal line.

Games are won and lost between the twenty-yard line and the goal line. To get across the goal line requires tenacity; it requires preparation, it requires impeccable strategy, it requires great sacrifice, it requires paying attention to every detail, and it requires a burning desire to win. If the church in little America is to start winning again, we have no choice but to go all in on getting across the goal line. Statistics and individuals are telling us that just getting our varsity letters or just kicking a field goal occasionally isn't getting the job done. We are losing, but the game is not over. There is hope, but if hope is to become reality, then the following elements need to become a part of our strategy.

The first is that we need to emphasize discipleship more than Christianity.

Up until the past year, I always saw the words *Christian* and *disciple* as synonyms. If you were a Christian, you were a disciple, and if you were a disciple, you were a Christian. I now see that the last part of that statement is true, but the first part is not. To realize this, we need to come to an agreed-upon definition for each of the words. Most everyone generally agrees that a good definition of a Christian is a follower of Jesus Christ. It was at Antioch that the followers of Christ first got their name of Christians. But what is the definition of a disciple? Here the Christian community is not as close in agreement. If you were to go to a conference on discipleship and the speaker were to ask you what the main purpose of the church is, there would be strong consensus that the main purpose of the church is to make disciples. But when the speaker then asks the question, "Okay, then what is a disciple?" there are likely to be fifty different definitions for fifty different people.

This was the problem when we started Thrive Ministries. We stated that our goal in forming this ministry was to be more effective in making disciples. We all patted ourselves on the back for being so biblical and then immediately went off in our own direction trying to make disciples not really knowing what we were trying to make. We were not unique in this. I know this because there is not strong agreement on what it means to be a disciple. For me, the picture became clear when I finally took the time to study the first words Jesus said to Peter and Andrew when he called them to be his disciples. We read these words in Matthew 4:19 (NIV): "'Come, follow me,' Jesus said, 'and I will send you out to fish for people.'"

In this command, Jesus clarifies the distinction between a Christian and a disciple. What is a Christian? One who follows Jesus. What is a disciple? According to these words of Jesus, a disciple is "a follower of Jesus who is being transformed by Jesus and is fully committed to the mission of Jesus." Let us look more closely at these words of Jesus.

First, he uses the word *follow*, and this word defines both a

Christian and a disciple. The gospels contain many references where Jesus personally invited people to follow him. The Greek word translated as "follow" in most of these references is *akoloutheō*. This is a common word and is used throughout the Greek New Testament but especially in the gospels.

While *akoloutheō* is almost always translated as "follow" in English translations, it has a broader range of meanings. It can also mean "accompany" and "assist." Many New Testament translations and lexicons do not give these other meanings; this is because they tend to favor the traditional translation of "follow." *Strong's*, however, is one lexicon that gives the extra meanings of "accompany" and "attend," as well as "follow."

If we understand that *akoloutheō* can have the meanings of "accompany" and "assist," as well as "follow," we can see that when Jesus was calling people to follow him, he wasn't just saying "tag along."

Jesus did not want people to just listen and believe in him from a distance. He was inviting people to come close, join him, and even help him with his mission. He wanted people to be vitally engaged with him in both learning and doing the work of the gospel.

For Jesus to simply tell Peter and Andrew seems like it would be enough. But when Jesus called the twelve to be his disciples, he let them know that to be a disciple required more than being a follower. Being a disciple also requires being willing to be transformed by Jesus. Jesus tells Peter and Andrew that he wants them to follow him, and then he tells them what else is required if they are going to be one of his disciples: their career focus was going to shift. Whereas before they were fishing for animals, now they were to be fishing for people. Whereas before they were spending a majority of their time in a boat on a lake, now they were going to be spending a majority of their time on a mission with their master. Whereas before, earthly investment would be the goal, now their goal would be heavenly investments. Whereas before they were in charge, now they would be under the charge of Jesus.

On a website I frequent because it is comprised entirely of sermon illustrations, an unnamed person said this about the present-day motor home:

> The motor home has allowed us to put all the conveniences of home on wheels. A camper no longer needs to contend with sleeping in a sleeping bag, cooking over a fire, or hauling water from a stream. Now he can park a fully equipped home on a cement slab amid a few pine trees and hook up to a water line, a sewer line and electricity. One motor home I saw recently had a satellite dish attached on top. No more bother with dirt, no more smoke from the fire, no more drudgery of walking to the stream. Now it is possible to go camping and never have to go outside. We buy a motor home with the hope of seeing new places, of getting out into the world. Yet we deck it out with the same furnishings as in our living room. Thus, nothing really changes. We may drive to a new place, set ourselves in new surroundings, but the newness goes unnoticed, for we've only carried along our old setting.

The picture of a disciple comes into focus when the comfortable patterns of the old life are left behind. Peter and James were not only being called to follow Jesus; they were being called to stop following the things from their old lives.

So to, when Jesus calls us to be his disciples, which he does, it is not only a matter of following him closely; it is a matter of no longer following the things of our former life. It is a matter of tearing down our old treasures and leaving them behind. It is a matter of deemphasizing and disbanding what may have been good for the sake of cherishing and embracing what is the best.

And finally, the picture of a disciple glows with full clarity when we are fully committed to the mission of Jesus Christ. What Jesus called Peter and Andrew to do was to join him in his mission. What was the mission of Jesus? To fish for people. What was the new mission of Peter and Andrew? To fish for people. What is our mission? To fish for people. How committed was Jesus to his mission? He was willing to die for it. How committed were Peter and Andrew to be their new mission? They were to be willing to die for it. How committed are we to be to our mission? We are to be willing to die for it.

See the difference between a Christian and a disciple? See why the words are not synonymous? See why if we are to cross the goal line, we need churches full of disciples and not just filled with Christians? Do not get me wrong. Christians are the recipients of salvation. Being a follower of Jesus Christ is our calling, and it is God's desire for all of us. Being a disciple is not a matter of works or righteousness. Being a disciple is not different than being a Christian, but being a disciple is what is necessary if the church is going to have maximum impact on our society and culture. Nothing has changed. Jesus needed disciples for his ministry to change the world, and he needs disciples today for his mission to change the world.

We need to emphasize sharing, connecting, and ministering over butts, bucks, and buildings.

It is here that I need to give credit to Jim Putnam and his book *DiscipleShift*. In this book, Putnam spends an entire section on the ingredients that signal whether a church is healthy and making a difference. For too many years, the health and impact of a church has been signified by the number of people in the pews, the level of giving of those butts, and the quality and size of the buildings where those butts are sitting. While these factors should not be ignored, they do not tell the whole story. To focus on butts, bucks, and buildings is to look at the scoreboard at a football game and look at everything but the most important thing: the score. The butts, bucks, and buildings can tell you how many yards a team has gained, how many first downs a team has made, how many time-outs a team has left, what yard line the ball is on, what down it is, how many yards are needed for a first down, and how much time is left in a quarter and a game and give a replay of what just happened. But even if we look at all these things on a scoreboard, we don't see who is winning. What are the most important numbers on a scoreboard? The number of points each team has.

For too long, the church in little America has been using the wrong scoreboard, and the result is that we have been falling further behind and we have not even noticed. We have counted our butts and bucks and looked at our buildings, but has that told us about how much we are impacting lives in our churches and community? It has told us how many people will be receiving their varsity letter. It has told us how much people are giving. And it has told us how much we care about our facilities. But has it told us anything about how well we are doing at making disciples who make disciples?

If the church in little America is going to start winning again, we need to get a new scoreboard. This new scoreboard does not need to be all that fancy or have all that many gadgets with it. This new scoreboard does not need to be expensive, state of the art, or cutting edge. This new scoreboard does not need to be changeable for every season. However, this new scoreboard does need to be large enough to get the attention of everyone. This new scoreboard needs to let us know when we get a win and how many are playing to win. This new scoreboard needs to send a consistent and constant message of how we are doing.

Here is a drawing of what I believe needs to be on the scoreboard of every church in little America. One, there needs to be a spot that tells us how many people are sharing their faith. In that spot are four spaces. One of the spaces tells us how many in our church have shared their faith with other believers in the past year, and another spot tells us how many have shared their faith with unbelievers in the past year. A third spot tells us how many were sharing their faith with believers two years ago, and the fourth one tells us how many were sharing their faith with unbelievers two years ago. How do we get this information? We ask our people through a short survey. Will it be completely accurate? No. Will it be enough to give us an idea? Probably. Will it remind people of how important it is that we are sharing our faith in the world? Absolutely.

Two, there needs to be a spot that tells us how many people in our church are connecting with people both in our churches and in our community. Once again, in that spot on the scoreboard, there are four numbers, the numbers connecting with believers in the past year, the number connecting with unbelievers in the past year, the number who were connecting with believers two years ago, and the number who were connecting with unbelievers two years ago.

What qualifies as connecting? Those who are consistently participating in a group with two to three others for the purpose of spiritual growth, those who are consistently participating in a small group of eight to ten others for spiritual growth, and those building relationships with unbelievers on a consistent basis.

Once again, how do we find out? We ask people. Will the information be completely accurate? No. Will the information be enough to give us a good idea of how we are doing? Probably. Will the question send the message of how important connecting with others is? Absolutely.

Three, there needs to be a spot that conveys how many people in our church are ministering to others on a consistent basis. What do we mean by ministering? We mean coming alongside people who are hurting and have needs of any kind. We mean loving our neighbor as illustrated by Jesus in his story about the Good Samaritan. We mean being so incarnate that people are seeing Jesus in us.

Like the other markers of sharing and connecting, we have four numbers. The first number is those who ministered to other believers in the past year. The second number is those who ministered to unbelievers in the past year. The third number is those who were ministering to other believers two years ago. And the fourth number is those who were ministering to unbelievers two years ago.

How do we find out? We ask. Will the numbers be completely accurate? No. Will the numbers give us a good idea of how we are doing and whether we are improving? They should. Will the question send the message of how important ministering to others is? Absolutely.

The fourth spot needs to be a place that tells us how many of our disciples have made other disciples. This is the most difficult of the numbers to quantify mainly because disciple-making is a marathon and not a sprint. This is also difficult to quantity because it is sometimes hard to know where the finish line is. This is also difficult to quantify because it is not a straight journey. Making other disciples is messy. Making other disciples often includes taking a step back after taking two steps forward. And making disciples can mean adapting from Plan A to Plan B or to Plan C. Still, this is a worthwhile number to have on the scoreboard because it sends a constant message of the necessity of disciples making other disciples if we are going to start winning again.

We need to emphasize the kingdom of God more than the local church.

To understand what it means to emphasize the kingdom of God requires an understanding of what the kingdom of God is. The kingdom of God is another of those terms used often in our Christian circles, and when we hear it, we nod and move on without really thinking about what we just heard or read. We are not going to do that right now, are we? We are going to pause for a second or two to at least get a broad understanding of what the kingdom of God is.

Jesus taught that where the King was, there was the kingdom. But he said much more. He clearly stated his objective. Immediately following his temptation, Jesus announced that objective. We read in Matthew 4:17 (NIV) that "from that time on Jesus began to preach, 'Repent, for the Kingdom of God is at hand.'" Immediately after the selection of the twelve, Jesus delivered the kingdom manifesto called the Sermon on the Mount. In that sermon, he explained who was great in the kingdom and could get into the kingdom, and later he offered the kingdom and told parables about it.

He told the disciples to pray for the kingdom, and when he sent them out, he told them to preach, "Repent for the Kingdom of God is at hand." He wept over Jerusalem because it had rejected the offer of the kingdom. He told the disciples that the kingdom was the place where the gospel was preached, which was all nations. At his ascension, they asked if now was the time that he would establish his kingdom.

When Jesus walked this earth, there were a lot of times when the kingdom was mentioned. When Jesus walked this earth, there were a lot of places where the kingdom was mentioned. When Jesus walked this earth, there were a lot of people who heard about the kingdom. So, what was Jesus talking about? The short answer is this: The kingdom of God is Jesus's rule in the world.

The rule of Jesus on this earth is separated into two phases. When Jesus first came to earth, he began what is best referred to as the inaugurated kingdom. What is meant by that? Well, what is the definition of inaugurate? The definition of *inaugurate* is to make a formal beginning of, to initiate, to commence. For example, "the end of World War II inaugurated the era of nuclear power."

When Jesus came to earth, there was a formal beginning of his rule in the world, it commenced. When a president is inaugurated, his term begins; it commences.

What is still coming is what can be referred to as the established or culminated kingdom. This will happen when Jesus returns for the second time. At this coming, there will be a new heaven and a new earth, and everything will be perfect. At this time, there will be no more pain, sorrow, crying, temptation, or sin. This is a time all believers look forward to.

In the meantime, in the here and now, where does the church fit into the kingdom of God? The first part of that answer is that the church exists for the kingdom of God. This is the "go into the word" part of the Great Commission. It is the responsibility of God's people to take the rule of Christ into the home, workplace, classroom, courthouse, and all facets of life and business. Just think of the impact the Christian community would have on our areas if we were faithfully doing just that. Why would all the segments of society change? Because dedicated disciples of Christ would not rest until it happened.

The second part of the answer to the question "Where does the church fit into the kingdom of God?" is that dedication to the church is not enough. We need to embrace this larger picture of the kingdom because without it, we too often think of the church as existing for itself. The church becomes an idol. "Commit yourself to it," we say. "Build it up," we say. "Make it the focal point of the experience," we say. And ... by so doing, we miss out on the big picture of the Great Commission.

I confess that for too many years, I and my colleagues have made church involvement the final goal, the top priority, and the goal line. I confess that for too many years, I and my colleagues have challenged church members to be pieces of the small puzzle of the local church rather than to be the corner pieces of the bigger puzzle that is the kingdom of God.

I confess that for too many years, I and my colleagues have not set out a big enough vision for the followers of Jesus Christ, that we have lowered the expectation that Jesus has for disciples, and that we have spent too much effort motivating our members to tasks that are too mundane, easy, and ordinary, and, yippee, our members have reached our expectations. For what? To brag that we have a large number of volunteers? How trivial compared to being able to brag that our church is making a difference in the arenas of our community. How trivial to boast about how many players we have on our team when we are not winning many games.

I confess that I and my colleagues have too often challenged our people to make it big in the church but not big in the world. We have told them that if they try hard, that if they work diligently and keep their noses clean, they can work their way up to a deacon or maybe even an elder. Is that the Great Commission that Jesus has called us to?

It is important to have dedicated servants and leaders within the church structure. But let us not mistake that for the reason the church exists. When Jesus calls us to be salt and light in the world, do we too often misinterpret that to mean salt and light in our churches? Dedication in the church itself is not enough if the church in little America is going to start winning again.

It makes me so sad that for too long as a pastor, I led God's people as if our mission field were inside our doors rather than outside our doors. It makes me so sad that for too long, I was more preoccupied with keeping the lives of the church members the same rather than focusing on making the lives of the people in the community better. It makes me so sad that far too often, our local churches were the teepees of our tribes rather than mission outposts for the hurting and oppressed.

Three pastors got together for coffee one day and found all their churches had bat-infestation problems. "I got so mad," said one, "I took a shotgun and fired at them. It made holes in the ceiling but did nothing to the bats."

"I tried trapping them alive," said the second. "Then I drove fifty miles before releasing them, but they beat me back to church."

"I haven't had any more problems," said the third.

"What did you do?" asked the others, amazed.

"I simply baptized and confirmed them," he replied. "I haven't seen one since."

Somehow, we, parishioners and pastors alike, need to get rid of the notion that once we get into the church, we have arrived, that once we get our varsity letter, we are good.

Some time ago, I heard a very well-meaning deacon make what came across as a positive statement. What did he say? He said, "I just want to have my own little church." As much as I appreciate the sentiment of that person and as much as I could see where he was coming from, I was so sad to hear the comment. "I just want to have my own little church" is the philosophy that is keeping the church in little America from winning. "I just want to have my own little church" is the mind-set that is holding the church back and keeping it from fulfilling the Great Commission. "I just want to have my own little church" is the attitude that keeps us stuck inside our church doors rather than going out into the world.

If the church in little America is going to start winning again, we need to stop prioritizing getting people into our church doors and into our pews and start prioritizing getting people outside of our church doors and into the world.

We need to emphasize relationships more than everything else.

Back in the 1970s, there was a game show called the *$10,000 Pyramid*. In this game, a celebrity and a contestant would play to guess the common thread that was given to them. For instance, if the category was "animals," one of the players would mention different animals until his or her teammate guessed the correct answer. Today, there is a gameshow with a similar idea. The gameshow is *America Says*, and a team of four guesses answers submitted by people in America related to a certain theme. For instance, if the theme is kinds of tables, the contestants, using the hint of the first letter of the answers, guesses what America said. So, there is a "c" and a blank line, and the answer is "coffee" table.

We now come to the portion of this book that is interactive. I am going to share a few situations, and I want you to guess the common theme that runs through all of them. All these situations have arisen in the last eighteen months. I do not know your IQs, but I am guessing that almost all of you will get the correct answer. I will give the clues in the reverse order of which I encountered the situation.

The first happened at a pastor/conference my wife and I recently attended. The speaker said that for churches to grow, the pastor needed to do four evangelistic activities. One of them is that he or she must spend five hours a week in the community and one of those hours is to be spent sharing the gospel.

The second happened at a virtual seminar I attended recently with a few of our church leaders. At the very beginning of the event, we were all told that the most important thing we must be doing is building relationships.

The third was a book I recently read written for pastors serving in rural areas. The author made the point that while in larger areas, the pastor needs to practice administrative leadership, in rural communities, the pastor needs to practice relational leadership.

The fourth was another conference I attended with church leaders that was a discipleship forum. There were several great speakers at this forum, and many of them shared that they were only speaking at this forum because there had been someone who reached out to them and built a relationship with them.

The fifth came from a get-together of the group of men I meet with every other week. The four of us had been studying a book that was challenging us to be the men we really wanted to be. The chapter that day as on our busyness and how it can affect our relationships. We were challenged to think about what relationships in our lives really suffer when we get too busy.

And here is the final clue. Last year, our board went through the book *The Master Plan of Evangelism* by Robert Coleman. If you know this classic book, you know that Coleman uses the example Jesus set with his disciples as the model for us to follow if we are going to change the world. One of the first and most important things Jesus did was to spend time with his disciples.

Okay, that should be enough clues. What is the common thread running through all these examples? If you guess the importance of relationships in reaching the world for Christ, then you are exactly right. However, you do not win for knowing the answer. Churches in little America are full of people who know the right answer. Churches in little America are full of people who know that relationships are important. Churches in little America are full of people who know the Bible talks extensively about our need to have a relationship with Jesus and relationships with others.

If knowing the right answer was the key to the church in little America winning, we would be undefeated. But here is why our record is not that great: while we know the answer, we are not putting the answer into practice. Winning does not come by gaining knowledge but by applying that knowledge.

That truth should be as clear as the nose on the front of our face, but somehow, we don't get it. Liberty Mutual has a commercial that uses a caricature artist to highlight the fact that this company offers plans that are individualized to each client. The artist finishes her portrait of the cameraman, who is eating a submarine sandwich and wearing a long-billed cap. The picture is an exaggerated spitting image of the guy, but when she shows it to him, he fails to see himself in the picture.

The church in little America is never going to win if we do not see the importance of relationships and that we are the keys to building those relationships. Our relationships with God and the people of our world need to be our number-one priority, but we are not pursuing this with enough zeal and vigor. Why not? Here are two possible reasons.

The first is that we do not know how. If we were to catch the vision of the couple in the "little" dream I shared earlier, how do we go about pursuing that dream? If we were to pray about people to ask and those people agreed to join with us, what happens next? If you are entertaining these two questions, you are not the first to entertain them. It may be just you and I who have ever stopped moving ahead because we were scared off by the lack of an answer to the questions, but at least we can we are not alone.

Here are my suggestions. Begin slowly. Begin by sharing your life stories. This may take the form of sharing five significant moments in your life, by sharing a time line of your spiritual journey, or by sharing the things that turn your crank and the things that stop you dead in your tracks, but start by opening up and letting others get a peek inside of your life.

The next step is to identify material to use when you get together. The choices here are endless.

You may want to use Christian books with discussion questions at either the end of the chapters or the end of the book. You may want to choose books that do not have discussion questions. In this case, all of you read a chapter each time, underline phrases that hit you, and then discuss those phrases. Or you highlight a phrase that you did not really understand, and then your group wrestles together with what the author meant. Or you share a thought that came to you while reading the chapter and ask the others what they think. Sometimes when we use a book with questions given to us, we can get a little scared, but there really isn't anything to fear. We all have different thoughts and questions that come to us when we engage in reading.

Another possibility is going right to the Bible and selecting a book or a chapter that all of you have an interest in. If you decide on this option, there is a plethora of study guides on the market to choose to augment your study. Personally, I prefer to forego the study guide, have the passage read a couple of times, and use the following set of questions for every passage you look at: What did we learn about God from this story? What did learn about humankind from this story? How could we use this story/passage to disciple someone? How can we apply this story in our own life? What is God asking me/us to do? It is amazing what comes out of a passage when these questions are used.

If you want to make it last longer, commit to memorizing a verse or two from the passage. We all have a tendency to balk when we are asked to memorize because most of think our memories are bad, and thus, we won't be able to accomplish our goal. My experience, however, is that most of us memorize better than we think, and even if we do not get the verses word for word, there is still great value in the effort to get the verse or verses memorized.

Throughout this stage of building relationships with other men or women, be praying for direction from God as to what he wants you to do when you finish your prearranged length of time for meeting. Maybe God will lead you to find something deeper to dig into. Hopefully, God will be putting it on your hearts to branch off and find others to be a part of a discipling relationship. When this happens, four become six or eight and ten or twelve and so on. The goal is to continue to multiply and do so by finding people who are either potential leaders or newcomers to the faith or people who just have an interest in spiritual matters.

And remember to have the best target in mind. Gaining information is a good target but not the best target. Having feel-good moments is a good target, but it is not the best target. Having a group that cares for each other is a good target, but it is not the best target. The ultimate target in these groups is growing to become people who are not only following the Lord, who are not only being transformed by the Lord, and who are not only committed to the mission of the Lord but disciples who are making other disciples who will in turn make their own disciples.

It is here that a parenthesis needs to be inserted. While groups of three or four are ideal, what is most important is that we let the Holy Spirit lead. It may be that God has put one specific person on your heart. If that is the case, go for it. Come alongside that person. Invest in that person. Get to know that person. If you are not sure what the conversation will look like, the internet is a great resource. There are sites you can go to that offer lists of leading questions to use to start conversations and bring depth and richness to the conversation. We cannot be too proud to use these resources. Many people have testimonies that point to one person who believed in them, talked with them, prayed with them, and walked with them.

The second reason we do not make relationships our number-one priority is that relationships are risky. My wife and I agree that the main reason we have not been fully committed to being disciples who make disciples is that we are afraid of what might happen when we head down this road. The first risk is that we may be rejected … and rejected … and rejected. We may be weird, but we prefer acceptance over rejection. None of us like hearing "no" from someone we invited to join us on a journey.

The second risk is that our invitation might be accepted. It has often been said that if it weren't for people, then building relationships would be a lot more enjoyable and a lot easier. I think we can agree that if you are reading this book, you do not have any negative personality traits. We are not the problem. The problem is that everyone else does. There are so many people out there who are high maintenance. There are so many people out there who are poor communicators. There are so many people out there who are carrying unhealthy baggage. There are so many people out there of a different political persuasion. There are so many people out there whose language makes us blush. There are so many people out there who do not have any tact. There are so many people out there who are not dependable. There are so many people out there who are too easily offended. There are even a few people out there who root for teams that we grew up hating. To that situation, I would say that there may be an exception to the rule of needing to build relationships. However, before you dismiss or disregard that person, you may want to talk to God about it.

The truth is that relationships, even the best ones, can often be messy. If you are married, think of your marriage. Has it always gone smoothly? Have there been times when you wanted to throw in the towel? Have there been times you wished you had listened to your mother and just remained single?

Think about it this way? Do you think Jesus always enjoyed the relationships he had with the twelve disciples? Do you think that Jesus often did not wish that Peter would just once think before he spoke? Do you think that Jesus did not want to bury his head in the sand when the mother of James and John asked if her sons could have special seats in heaven? Do you think that Jesus did not want to yell at them when they did not catch on to what he was teaching them? Do you think that Jesus did not want to cry when the three closest to him did not stay awake when he went up to the Mount of Olives to pray? Do you think Jesus did not want to cringe every time he saw Judas because he knew what was in Judas's heart? Do you think Jesus did not want to give up when Thomas, and others, needed more evidence that he was who he said he was?

But what would have happened if Jesus has given up on the twelve? What if Jesus had determined that building relationships with these guys was not worth the hassle? What if Jesus had aborted the mission because these guys were not making the progress he was hoping for? What if Jesus had come to the point where he could only see them as they were and not what they were going to become with the help of his Father in heaven?

Investing in other people is risky, but if the church in little America is going to win again, it is necessary. If we are going to start getting to the goal line instead of only the fifty-yard line, we need to be committed to getting in groups with others and challenging each other to want more than to just earn our varsity letter to present to God as our ticket to getting into heaven. If we are going to put points on the scoreboard, it will only happen when we start our sharing our faith more frequently with other believers and people in our communities.

If we are going to start making an impact on the playing fields of our towns and villages, we need to start connecting with more believers and with more people in our communities. Staying on the sidelines or just stepping onto the field for a play or two is not going to cut it. Standing outside the locker room believing that if we simply open the doors and let the team through, we will win is to be trapped in the thinking of a previous millennium and a previous generation.

If we are going to win on a consistent basis, we need to be out ministering to the needs of the people in our communities. We need to be searching out the poor, the suicidal, the oppressed, the enslaved, the addicted, the immoral, and the ignored. And when we get to them, we need to extend a listening ear and a portion of our time. When we get to them, we need to be their friends. When we get to them, we need to be willing to receive their ten texts a day or their zero texts in a week. When we get to them, we need to be willing to love them for who they are rather than for who we want them to be. When we get to them, we can't be afraid to tell about the difference Jesus has made in our lives. When we get to them, we can't be turned away by how they smell, how they talk, how they perceive the world, or their victim mentality.

For the church in little America to start winning again, we must stop living in our yesterdays and start claiming our tomorrows. For the church in little America to start winning again, we have to stop recounting the number of kids who were in our Sunday schools in the 1960s and 1970s and start counting the number of people in our rehab centers and in our jails and in our soup lines. We need to start counting the number of kids who have no one to go home to after school. We need to start counting the number of teens who are looking for acceptance in promiscuous relationships because they are not being accepted at love. We need to start counting the families using the food pantry each week. And we need to start counting the number of elderly who don't have anyone who comes to visit them.

For the church in little America to start winning again, we need to start expecting more of our team. Getting people into the doors of our church on Sunday mornings can no longer be the bar we set. The bar needs to be set at how many unbelievers are coming to know Jesus and then leading others to come to know Jesus. The bar needs to be set at how many disciples are we making who are then making other disciples. When this starts happening, we will start winning again. When this starts happening, the influence and allure of the world will begin to wane and the beauty of the church will begin to wax. When this starts happening, the division of Christian and non-Christian will become smaller, and we will begin to see again the great truth that we are created in the image of God and that for the grace of God, we would all be in the same place.

2

GAME PLAN AGAINST THE OPPONENT

We need to game plan against the opponent.

The Jordan Rules were a successful defensive basketball strategy employed by the Detroit Pistons against Michael Jordan to limit his effectiveness on the game. Devised by Isiah Thomas in 1988, the Pistons' strategy was "to play him tough, to physically challenge him and to vary its defenses so as to try to throw him off balance." Sometimes, the Pistons would overplay Jordan to keep the ball from him. Sometimes they would play him straight up. More often, they would run a double team at him as soon as he touched the ball to try to force him to give it up. And whenever he went to the basket, they made sure his path was contested. They forced him to go left, which he was less successful in doing. Additionally, whomever Jordan was guarding on defense, Detroit would force the basketball to the player Jordan was guarding to make him work extremely hard on both ends of the court, thus rendering him less effective.

Jordan began his playoff career with three consecutive first-round exits (none by Detroit), followed up by one exit in the second round and two in the Eastern Conference Championship (all by Detroit), and then won three consecutive titles before retiring for a year.

This strategy has also sometimes been employed against other prolific scoring guards. The Jordan Rules were an instrumental aspect of the rivalry between the "Bad Boys" Pistons and Jordan's Chicago Bulls in the late 1980s and early 1990s. This style of defense limited players, including Jordan, from entering the paint and was carried out by Dennis Rodman and Bill Laimbeer.

The Jordan Rules were most effective for the Pistons during their first three playoff meetings with the Bulls. Detroit beat Chicago four games to one in the 1988 Eastern Conference Semifinals. The Pistons and Bulls met each other in the NBA Eastern Conference Finals for the next three seasons. Detroit's defense defeated the Bulls in six games in 1989 and in seven games in 1990. The Pistons won back-to-back championships after eliminating the Bulls. Finally, in 1991, the Bulls defeated the Pistons in the playoffs, neutralizing the Jordan Rules with their triangle offense orchestrated by Coach Phil Jackson and assistant Tex Winter.

In an interview with *Sports Illustrated*, then Detroit Pistons coach Chuck Daly described the Jordan Rules as "If Michael was at the point, we forced him left and doubled him. If he was on the left wing, we went immediately to a double team from the top. If he was on the right wing, we went to a slow double team. He could hurt you equally from either wing—he could hurt you from the hot-dog stand—but we just wanted to vary the look. And if he was on the box, we doubled with a big guy. The other rule was, any time he went by you, you had to nail him. If he was coming off a screen, nail him. We didn't want to be dirty—I know some people thought we were—but we had to make contact and be very physical."

When doing an ESPN 30 for 30, Joe Dumars said, "It goes, the Da Vinci Code, the recipe to Coca-Cola, then the Jordan Rules" (Wikipedia).

The Chicago Bulls had the best player, but the Detroit Pistons had the best game plan, and the end result was that the Detroit Pistons were the winners. The Pistons knew that the way to win was to game plan against the opponent's best player, and if that player could be slowed down, the chances of winning increased dramatically.

The church in little America needs to mimic the strategy of the Detroit Pistons. We need to identify the strength of the opponent and game plan against that opponent. If the church in little America is going to start winning again, we need to game plan against the two following opponents: self and Satan.

We all know that once we become a believer, the battle is not over; it is just beginning in earnest. The internal civil war between good and evil and right and wrong is best articulated by the Apostle Paul in Romans 7:15–25 (NIV):

> I do not understand what I do. For what I want to do I do not do, but what I hate I do. And if I do what I do not want to do, I agree that the law is good. As it is, it is no longer I myself who do it, but it is sin living in me. For I know that good itself does not dwell in me, that is, in my sinful nature. For I have the desire to do what is good, but I cannot carry it out. For I do not do the good I want to do, but the evil I do not want to do—this I keep on doing. Now if I do what I do not want to do, it is no longer I who do it, but it is sin living in me that does it. So I find this law at work: Although I want to do good, evil is right

there with me. For in my inner being I delight in God's law; but I see another law at work in me, waging war against the law of my mind and making me a prisoner of the law of sin at work within me. What a wretched man I am! Who will rescue me from this body that is subject to death? Thanks be to God, who delivers me through Jesus Christ our Lord! So then, I myself in my mind am a slave to God's law, but in my sinful nature a slave to the law of sin.

And to think that this was his struggle after, not before, his conversion! I relate to that struggle, and I guess that many of you do as well. So, how do we go about fighting this battle against our sinful natures?

A great way to defeat self is by fasting. The importance of fasting is that fasting is an act of surrender to our wills and a statement that God's will is more important than ours. Once again I go to the website 'Sermon Illustrations" where we find a man named Dan Allender saying this: "Fasting from any nourishment, activity, involvement or pursuit—for any season—sets the stage for God to appear."

Several books have been written on fasting by people who know more about this than I do. What I am going to do is share the four reasons why fasting needs to be practiced more often in the church in little America. Fasting is the most underutilized weapon at our disposal. These are the breakthroughs that will happen when we start using this tool with more diligence and regularity.

First, *fasting sensitizes us to the Holy Spirit*. In the New Testament, there is what can be called the threefold cord of normal Christian duty. This cord consists of giving, praying, and fasting. Solomon, when writing the books of wisdom for Israel, made the point that a cord, or rope, braided with three strands is not easily broken. Likewise, when giving, praying, and fasting are practiced together in the life of a believer, it creates a type of threefold cord that is not easily broken. In fact, Jesus took it even further by saying in Matthew 12:26 (NIV), "With man this is impossible, but with God all things are possible."

Could we be missing our greatest breakthroughs because we fail to fast? In Mark 4:8 and 20, Jesus speaks of a thirtyfold, sixtyfold, and hundredfold return. Look at it this way: when we pray, we can release that thirtyfold return, but when both prayer and giving are part of our life, that releases the sixtyfold blessing. But when all three—giving, praying, and fasting—are part of our life, that hundredfold return can be released.

If that is the case, we must wonder what blessings are not being released. What answers to prayer are not getting through? What bondages are not being broken because we fail to fast? Or think of it this way: If Jesus could have accomplished all He came to do without fasting, why would he fast? The Son of God fasted because he knew there were supernatural things that could only be released that way. So how much more should fasting be a common practice in our lives?

In the Old Testament, the prophet speaks to this breakthrough. These are his words from Joel 2:12–17 and 28–29 (NIV):

> "Even now," declares the Lord, "return to me with all your heart, with fasting and weeping and mourning." Rend your heart and not your garments. Return to the Lord your God, for he is gracious and compassionate, slow to anger and

abounding in love, and he relents from sending calamity. Who knows? He may turn and relent and leave behind a blessing—grain offerings and drink offerings for the Lord your God. Blow the trumpet in Zion, declare a holy fast, call a sacred assembly. Gather the people, consecrate the assembly; bring together the elders, gather the children, those nursing at the breast. Let the bridegroom leave his room and the bride her chamber. Let the priests, who minister before the Lord, weep between the portico and the altar. Let them say, "Spare your people, Lord. Do not make your inheritance an object of scorn, a byword among the nations. Why should they say among the peoples, "Where is their God?"

"And afterward, I will pour out my Spirit on all people. Your sons and daughters will prophesy, your old men will dream dreams, your young men will see visions. Even on my servants, both men and women, I will pour out my Spirit in those days."

In verses 28 and 29 of Joel 2, God says he was going to pour out revival—afterward. He was revealing his will for his people—afterward. After what? After a fast. Israel was in sin, and God was calling his people to fast in repentance as a people: "Blow the trumpet in Zion, consecrate a fast, call a sacred assembly."

His promise to them was to pour out revival and blessings on the land. The message is clear in Joel 2: after fasting the people of Israel dreamed *dreams* and saw *visions.* This was not about a coincidence but about a connection. The scriptures are clear, through teaching and examples, that when we fast, we become more sensitive to the voice and leadings of the Holy Spirit.

If the promise of God and the example in the scripture is that fasting raises our sensitivity to the leading of the Spirit, is there any reason why any of us would continue to leave the tool of fasting in the shed when that is the precise tool needed to bring about the breakthroughs we are looking for?

So, what will we see? I know this ... I do not know. And that is what makes fasting a step of faith. If we already knew what we were going to see, why would we need to fast? This is what makes using this tool so exciting: we do not know what is on the other side of the wall that fasting helps us break through. It is why the more we study this truth and the more we practice this truth, the more convinced we will be that this is exactly what needs to become more and more a part of the DNA of the church in little America.

But this comes with a word of warning: we must be patient and not rush the process. This story from the school days of a Christian writer drives this point home. One year in elementary school, the teacher told him and his class to save their milk cartons from lunch. They were to bring them back to class where they were rinsed and had the funny tops cut off. She then opened a big container of black potting soil, and the class scooped some into their cartons. She handed the students a big butter bean seed and told them how to plant the seed in the soil by making a small hole with a finger and dropping the seed in. After the seed was watered and names were taped to the boxes, the students set their boxes in the sunny window.

Every day when the class started, young man ran to the window with the others to see what was happening with the seeds. Nothing happened until the third day when a tiny bit of green sprout began to show in some of the boxes. By day six, most of the boxes had green sprouts showing, and some even had leaves. But for the young man ... nothing. On the seventh day, he could take it no longer and used his finger to dig around in the soil to see if his seed was still in the box. Sure enough, after he pulled it out, he saw that it had begun to sprout.

You know the rest of the story. Because the young man had pulled out the seed too soon, he had destroyed the harvest. Fasting will bring a harvest, but it may take some time. We cannot become impatient, rush the process, and destroy the harvest. Rather, we need to trust God to bring the blessings he promises when we surrender to him.

Two, *fasting gets us where God wants us to be.* Our reference point for this truth is Ezra 8:15–23 (NIV):

> I assembled them at the canal that flows toward Ahava, and we camped there three days. When I checked among the people and the priests, I found no Levites there. So I summoned Eliezer, Ariel, Shemaiah, Elnathan, Jarib, Elnathan, Nathan, Zechariah and Meshullam, who were leaders, and Joiarib and Elnathan, who were men of learning, and I ordered them to go to Iddo, the leader in Kasiphia. I told them what to say to Iddo and his fellow Levites, the temple servants in Kasiphia, so that they might bring attendants to us for the house of our God. Because the gracious hand of our God was on us, they brought us Sherebiah, a capable man, from the descendants of Mahli son of Levi, the son of Israel, and Sherebiah's sons and brothers, 18 in all; and Hashabiah, together with Jeshaiah from

the descendants of Merari, and his brothers and nephews, 20 in all. They also brought 220 of the temple servants—a body that David and the officials had established to assist the Levites. All were registered by name.

There, by the Ahava Canal, I proclaimed a fast, so that we might humble ourselves before our God and ask him for a safe journey for us and our children, with all our possessions. I was ashamed to ask the king for soldiers and horsemen to protect us from enemies on the road, because we had told the king, "The gracious hand of our God is on everyone who looks to him, but his great anger is against all who forsake him." So we fasted and petitioned our God about this, and he answered our prayer.

Many, many churches in little America are at a crossroad, and knowing which direction God wants us to take will go a long way in determining what our futures will look like. We are, thus, in the same place as the people of Israel were in this passage from Ezra. Here is the situation. The memory of Ezra the scribe has scarcely had fair play among Bible-reading people. True, neither his character nor the incidents of his life reach the height of interest or of grandeur belonging to the earlier men and their times. He is no hero or prophet, only a scribe, and there is a certain narrowness as well as a prosaic turn about his mind. Altogether, one feels that he is a smaller man than the Elijahs and Davids of the older days. But the homely garb of the scribe covered a very brave and devout heart, and the story of his life deserves to be more familiar to us than it is.

This scrap from the account of his preparations for the march from Babylon to Jerusalem gives us a glimpse of a high-toned faith and a noble strain of feeling. He and his company had a long, weary journey of four months before them. They had had little experience of arms and warfare or of hardships and desert marches in their Babylonian homes. Their caravan was made unwieldy and feeble by the presence of a large proportion of women and children. They had much valuable property with them.

The stony desert, which stretches unbroken from the Euphrates to the uplands on the east of the Jordan River, was infested then as now by wild bands of marauders, who might easily swoop down on the encumbered march of Ezra and his men and make a clean sweep of all that they had. And he knew that he had but to ask and have an escort from the king that would ensure their safety until they saw Jerusalem.

Artaxerxes's surname, "the long-handed," may have described a physical peculiarity, but it also expressed the reach of his power; his arm could reach these wandering plunderers, and if Ezra and his troop were visibly under his protection, they could march secure. So, it was not a small exercise of trust in a higher Hand that is told us here so simply. It took some strength of principle to abstain from asking what it would have been so natural to ask, so easy to get, so comfortable to have. But, as he says, he remembered how confidently he had spoken of God's defense, and he felt that he must be true to his professed creed, even if it deprived him of the king's guards.

He halted his followers for three days at the last station before the desert, and there, with fasting and prayer, they put themselves in God's hand. Then the band, with their wives and little ones and their substance—a heavily loaded and feeble caravan—flung themselves into the dangers of the long, dreary, robber-haunted march. Did not the scribe's robe cover as brave a heart as ever beat beneath a breastplate?

That is the picture I want you to keep in your mind as I now bring us to see the principle in this drawing. The principle begins with a sentence that begins this way: Fasting leads to humility. It is significant that Ezra 8:21 starts this way: "I proclaimed a fast so that we might humble ourselves …" If you are like me and know what I know about fasting, we would presume the sentence would start this way: "We humbled ourselves so that we might fast." Do you see the difference? If we read it the way we may presume it to be read, we would come to the conclusion that before we can fast, we need to humble ourselves. There is an element of truth here, but the greater truth is in the way it is actually written. The way Ezra describes it, the people fasted so that they would become humble. What leads to what? Does humility lead to fasting or does fasting lead to humility? According to this picture, fasting leads to humility.

What we also see in Ezra 8 is that not only does fasting lead to humility, but humility then leads to dependence on God. I'm afraid that too often our prayers take on the following tone: "Lord, we just want to let you know we are going to do this. Would you be kind enough to bless our decision?" Fasting will be the tool that gets us to the point where instead of us telling God what we are going to do, we let God tell us what he wants us to do.

Remember here that Ezra could have asked the king to go with the people on the journey, but Ezra decided against it. He was leading the people to realize that they needed to get to the point where they would no longer depend on the things in the world but could trust completely in God. Proverbs 3:5 (NIV) comes to my mind when I see this: "Trust in the Lord with all your heart and lean not on your own understanding."

What will fasting do? Fasting will lead us to a point where we surrender our future journey to him knowing that we will not be taking the journey alone. Do not get me wrong. There is a place in the life of a Christian for counselors and consultants. They fulfill a purpose, and many times, they are the instruments God provides to give us the help we need in going forward. But sometimes, like in the times our churches are facing right now, I believe that we need to be depending on God completely.

A sign seen in a textile mill said this, "When your thread becomes tangled, call the foreman." A young woman was new on the job. Her thread became tangled, and she thought, *I'll just straighten this out myself.* She tried, but the situation only worsened. Finally, she called the foreman. "I did the best I could," she said.

"No, you didn't. To do the best, you should have called me."

If we listen closely and think clearly, how many of us have not heard God saying the same thing to us?

This, then, leads to next phrase: dependence on God leads to *protection* and *direction*. When I first studied this passage, I struggled a little bit with the end of verse 21 because different Bibles translate the words differently. The NIV translates the words "and ask him for a safe journey" while other translations translate the words along the lines of seeking a right way. Because of the difference, I waffled for a while on how to best interpret this. Does it mean that when we humble ourselves before God, he protects us on our journeys or that when we humble ourselves before God, he directs us on our journey? The answer I settled on is "yes." When we humble ourselves before God, he gives us both protection and direction.

We fast because we need to know the right way for our lives. We do not need to be confused as to our future or the choices before us. Fast, seek his face, and have faith he will guide you. This is so biblical. In Judges 20:26, we see Israel seeking to know if they should go into battle against the tribe of Benjamin. In 1 Samuel 7:6, we see Israel seeking God at Mizpah for forgiveness and protection against the Philistine army. And in 2 Chronicles 20:3, we find Jehoshaphat inquiring about the army that was about to attack. God is a God who will give us protection and direction when we humble ourselves before him and put our faith in him.

This leads to the final truth about fasting in this passage. Fasting leads to humility, which then leads to dependence on God, which then leads to direction and protection, which then (direction and protection) bring us to where he wants us to be.

We read this in verse 23 (NIV): "So we fasted and petitioned our God about this, and he answered our prayer." A few verses later, we see that that God heard and answered their prayers. Fasting with prayer just seems to open a different frequency in God's ear. Ezra recorded that they left the river Ahava after twelve days to set out for Jerusalem. He also testified, "The hand of our God was on us, and he protected us from enemies and bandits along the way" (8:31 NIV). God's hand was upon them, his right hand protecting them and their little ones.

After years in exile, after years in a foreign land, God got the people back. Based on what God did for his people in this story, do you believe that if the church in little America will diligently fast, that God will get us back to winning again?

Three, *fasting makes us pliable*. To see this truth illustrated and explained we go to Mark 2:18–22 (NIV):

> Now John's disciples and the Pharisees were fasting. Some people came and asked Jesus, "How is it that John's disciples and the disciples of the Pharisees are fasting, but yours are not?" Jesus answered, "How can the guests of the

bridegroom fast while he is with them? They cannot, so long as they have him with them. But the time will come when the bridegroom will be taken from them, and on that day they will fast. "No one sews a patch of unshrunk cloth on an old garment. Otherwise, the new piece will pull away from the old, making the tear worse. And no one pours new wine into old wineskins. Otherwise, the wine will burst the skins, and both the wine and the wineskins will be ruined. No, they pour new wine into new wineskins.

In this story, we can believe here that Jesus is still in the home of Levi, or Matthew, whom he has just called to be his disciple. The Pharisees have seen him there, and now they are witnessing him with this motley crew feasting on a day when they, possibly, were fasting. Reading between the lines, we can see it is likely that this event was taking place on one of the weekly fast days.

Here is a little background regarding the practice of fasting. The only time we find a compulsory fast ordered in the Old Testament is for the Day of Atonement, Yom Kippur, when the Jews were commemorating the day when their sins were forgiven and, hopefully, by faith, looking to God for forgiveness of sins. But fasting had evolved to the stage where in Jesus's day, the stricter Jews fasted twice in a week: Monday and Thursday from 6:00 a.m. to 6:00 p.m. So, after 6:00 p.m., they could eat all they wanted. In Luke 18:12 (NIV), in the parable of the Pharisee and the publican, a tax collector, you remember that the Pharisee declared, self-righteously, "I fast twice in the week." So this was a common practice of the Pharisees and of their followers.

Jesus's protest here, that throws him into the midst of this controversy with the Pharisees and the disciples of John, is at the abuse of the practice of fasting among Jews in his day. You see it was exercised in an ostentatious way. What do I mean by that? I'll just quote for you the words of our Lord in the Sermon on the Mount in Matthew 6. He takes up more than just fasting, giving alms, and praying and how they were done hypocritically. In verse 1 he says"'Take heed,' that you do not practice your righteousness before men, to be seen of them: otherwise you have no reward of your Father which is in heaven.'" Matthew 6:6 says, "But you, when you pray, enter into your closet, and when you have shut the door, pray to thy Father which is in secret; and your Father which sees in secret shall reward you openly." Then, related to fasting in verses 16 to 18 of chapter 6 of Matthew, we read,

> Moreover when you fast, be not, as the hypocrites, of a sad countenance: for they disfigure their faces, that they may appear unto men to fast. Verily I say unto you, they have their reward. But thou, when you fast, anoint your head, and wash your face; so that you appear not unto men to fast, but unto your Father which is in secret: and your Father, which sees in secret, shall reward you openly. (Matthew 6:16–18 NIV)

Fasting that is done for the sake of telling people how spiritual we are renders the practice ineffective and, in fact, ugly to God. Jesus promoted fasting but only when the motivation was to direct our own attention to God. This is the motivation for fasting that God will honor and bless.

While it may be hard to see the correlation between wineskins and fasting in verses 21 and 22, it is there. And here is where it is. Thanks to the legalism that was imposed by the Pharisees, the Jewish religion in many respects had become a burdensome and joyless thing. These poor Jewish people were crushed by rules and regulations that Jesus himself even said were impossible to obey. To enforce this point and hammer it home, the Lord Jesus uses three illustrations to contrast dead, legalistic, mournful religious form with the living liberty of the joy of grace that is found in him.

One illustration is a wedding, one is a piece of clothing, and the last is a wineskin. It is the illustration of the wineskin that is most relevant for this chapter. We read about this in Joshua 9:4–13. They would take a goat. They would kill the goat, take the hide of the goat, use the neck as a spout, sew up the places where the legs were and any openings, and then they would have a big, big goatskin kind of pouch, fresh leather, and they would fill it with new wine.

They would leave it there for a period, and the bitterness of the dregs would go to the bottom and settle in the bottom, and they would pour it out of one skin into another new skin. And they would keep pouring it and pouring it. And each time they would pour it—they would do this time and time again—more of the dregs would be out and remain in the bottom. From that, they would make vinegar and things like that. But eventually, they would get a clear wine with no dregs left. That was the process. It was important that these skins be supple and that they be able to contain the wine.

If you had old skins lying around that had been used and reused and then not used for a period, they would crack. They would become brittle, and when they were used again, they would break open. All the wine would be lost. This was imagery they would completely understand. This was something they were familiar with. They would just keep pouring it until the bottom was clear, no dregs were left, and they had the pure wine that they were after.

Now, what is the message in all of this? The religion of the Pharisees and the scribes, the religion of the disciples of John, that was old skin; it could not contain the gospel. But rather than believe, rather than receive, they kept their dead, brittle, tattered old wineskins, and they refused the gospel.

Jesus said it is very natural for people to hang on to their familiar religion. The Jews had their old and ancient traditions, passed down generation to generation to generation to generation, father to son, on and on and on and on, so deeply ingrained. All the rituals, all the ceremonies, all the behaviors to which they had clung so tightly, they did not release them easily. It had become such a part of their lives. They had cultivated such a taste for their own religion that if you offered them something else, they were not interested in it. But we are not like that, are we? None of us cling to the old and the past because that is what is most comfortable, do we? None of us are stuck in the molds of what our Christian lives have always been like even if we are not bearing any fruit, are we? None of us are in bondage to a lukewarmness that makes us blend in with the rest of the world, are we?

And here is the connection with fasting. Fasting leads to humility. Humility then, as it relates to Mark 2:22, leads to pliable hearts. Pliable hearts then are the means through which God does greater things in us than we would ever imagine. Pliable hearts are the vessels into which God can pour out more of his blessings than could ever fit in an inflexible, nonexpanding heart. Pliable hearts are the avenues on which God delivers the abundant life that God wants for all of us.

Finally, *fasting brings about victories.* Mark 9 is a chapter that covers a lot of territory and illustrates many biblical truths.

The conclusion of the chapter is no exception. The disciples have had a "we couldn't do it" moment with a man who was possessed by a demon. A little later, Jesus comes down the Mount of Transfiguration, drives out the demon himself, and then engages in a conversation with them about why they could not do it. Verses 28 and 29 (NIV) give the explanation: "After Jesus had gone indoors, his disciples asked him privately, 'Why couldn't we drive it out?' He replied, 'This kind can come out only by prayer.'"

What is also added in many manuscripts, and rightfully so, is that not only was prayer needed but also fasting. The two go hand in hand because both speak to the need of surrendering to God and relying on him. Prayer is a state of close communion with the Lord. Fasting is a lifestyle of submission and surrender to the Lord. The disciples were not communing with God as they should have been. Neither were they as surrendered to God as they should have been. As a result, they lacked the power of God in their lives, and thus they could not cast out this demon.

The disciples did not fail because they did not believe. They believed all right, or they would not have tried to cast out the demon in the first place. Their problem was that they believed in the wrong things. They failed because their faith was in their words and the rituals they used and not in God. The disciples failed because they were not leaning on the Lord Jesus Christ for the power they needed. The truth here is that the more we give up, the more God gives out. The truth is that the more we crucify the self, the more we will celebrate the Christ.

If the church in little America is going to start winning again, we need to game plan against our sinful natures. If we are going to start winning again, we need to be willing to die to self. If we are going to start winning again, we need to get to the point where we surrender and submit ourselves and lean into the Lord. The tool to use to get to that point is fasting. Fasting is the most useful spiritual discipline in our toolbox for surrendering to God because fasting makes us say "no" to self and "yes" to God. It is fasting that makes us humble and pliable in the hands of God. When we are humble and pliable, we free up God to get us where he wants us to be and then give us victories that are unattainable in our own strength.

Before moving on, I would be remiss not to highlight the words of God in Isaiah 58 about the effect of true fasting. These are those words as shared from the NIV Bible:

> Shout it aloud, do not hold back. Raise your voice like a trumpet. Declare to my people their rebellion and to the descendants of Jacob their sins. For day after day they seek me out; they seem eager to know my ways, as if they were a nation that does what is right and has not forsaken the commands of its God. They ask me for just decisions and seem eager for God to come near them. Why have we fasted,'" they say, "and you have not seen it? Why have we humbled ourselves, and you have not noticed?" "Yet on the day of your fasting, you do as you please and exploit all your workers. Your fasting ends in quarreling and strife, and in striking each other with wicked fists. You cannot fast as you do today and expect your voice to be heard on high. Is this the kind of fast I have chosen, only a day for people to humble themselves? Is it only for bowing one's head like a reed and for lying in sackcloth and ashes? Is that what you call a fast, a day acceptable to the LORD? "Is not this the kind

of fasting I have chosen: to loose the chains of injustice and untie the cords of the yoke, to set the oppressed free and break every yoke? Is it not to share your food with the hungry and to provide the poor wanderer with shelter—when you see the naked, to clothe them, and not to turn away from your own flesh and blood? Then your light will break forth like the dawn, and your healing will quickly appear; then your righteousness will go before you, and the glory of the LORD will be you rear guard." Then you will call, and the LORD will answer; you will cry for help, and he will say: Here am I. "If you do away with the yoke of oppression, with the pointing finger and malicious talk, and if you spend yourselves on behalf of the hungry and satisfy the needs of the oppressed, then your light will rise in the darkness, and your night will become like the noonday. (Isaiah 58:1–10 NIV)

It is a bit hard to pin down exactly to whom these exhortations of Isaiah in this last section of the book, chapters 56 through 66, pertain specifically, for they could refer to God's captive people in Babylon who have been told that the Lord is going to bring their deliverer and return them to their land where they will restore their temple, city, and city wall. The encouragements and admonishments in this case would be for them to try to live as much within the Law of Moses as they can. Seeing the fact that they are living as slaves in Babylon, they do not have a temple in which they can sacrifice, and they do not have a priesthood with which to mediate their sacrifices. An attitude of heart is primarily what the people would be admonished to have since the literal keeping of many of the laws to the letter would be impossible.

From my studying, I believe the more likely audience is God's people after their restoration from captivity in Babylon when they are living in a rebuilt Jerusalem and with a rebuilt temple and priesthood.

The encouragements and admonishments in this case would be that since Isaiah has revealed that God's "ideal servant" will come and provide for the atonement for their sins and transgressions and since they now have their temple and priesthood functional, that they are to live as much as possible in faithful obedience to the law of God as they await the arrival of God's "ideal servant."

What we learn from verses 6 through 10 is that fasting with the right motivation will lead us to serving others. In verse 5, we see that the Israelites were going through the external motions of a fast, acting like they were humble, bowing their heads, spreading out sackcloth and ashes as a bed, and so on. However, in their hearts, they were truly not humble, and they were not seeking to have the Lord show them how and help them to really align their lives with him and his will for their lives.

The real purposes we, God's people, should have for fasting are recorded beginning in verse 6: to loosen the bonds of wickedness, to undo the bands of the yoke, to let the oppressed go free, to break every yoke, to divide our bread with the hungry and bring the homeless poor into the house.

None of the purposes the Lord gives for fasting are about us trying to manipulate the Lord to do our bidding, but rather, they are for us to get our hearts right with him and his true program for our life. This is the real value of fasting. We do not need to try to manipulate the Lord to do our will; we instead need to realize that God has a perfect plan that he is wanting to accomplish here on earth and through our lives, and we just need to get ourselves in proper relationship with him and thus in line with his plans for us and to use us.

Two, *we need to game plan against Satan.* It is always wise to go to Ephesians 6 when we are talking about spiritual warfare. As a reminder, here it is:

> Finally, be strong in the Lord and in his mighty power. Put on the full armor of God, so that you can take your stand against the devil's schemes. For our struggle is not against flesh and blood, but against the rulers, against the authorities, against the powers of this dark world and against the spiritual forces of evil in the heavenly realms. Therefore put on the full armor of God, so that when the day of evil comes, you may be able to stand your ground, and after you have done everything, to stand. Stand firm then, with the belt of truth buckled around your waist, with the breastplate of righteousness in place, and with your feet fitted with the readiness that comes from the gospel of peace. In addition to all this, take up the shield of faith, with which you can extinguish all the flaming arrows of the evil one. Take the helmet of salvation and the sword of the Spirit, which is the word of God. (Ephesians 6:10–17 NIV)

In addition to being faithful in putting on the full armor of God, we need to be faithful practicing what I call "combat prayer." The reason we need to actively engage in combat prayer is because Satan and his demons are present and prevalent in little America. I would not have made that statement years ago.

For the first thirty years of my life, I thought that demons were either only active in the days when Jesus walked this earth, or they only took up residence in other countries or big cities.

I really do not know why I was so naïve to believe this, but nevertheless, this was my belief. I have since made a 180-degree turn on this. Experiences in life will do just that. It started one Maundy Thursday when I was serving Communion to the members of my church at that time, and a woman came forward who literally had fire in her eyes. If the fire had not been so vivid, I would not have noticed because I normally didn't look for those things. But it was so clear, and it was unlike anything I had ever seen before.

From there, the exposure to Satan and his demons has just continued. There was the little rural mission we visited for a second time in our lives. The first time, it was a happy place. The second time, it was a dark place. My wife and I could feel the darkness coming down on us as we entered the gates of that mission. There was the rural area of a state we drove through. The rest of the state was beautiful, and this part of the state probably was as well, but we could not see it through the heaviness that permeated the air. Once again, the unexplainable feel of a horde of demons was unmistakable to us.

There were the issues we had with one of our children. We adopted him from a country that was littered with witchcraft and Satanism, and the demons that attached themselves to him in that country were brought back to our home. Many were the nights when our son would be pounding on the walls in his room, and we were unable to console and comfort him until we spoke against the demons in the name of Jesus. When that happened, the pounding would suddenly stop.

There are the constant Saturday nights of trying to memorize my sermons and the demonic harassment that I can count on—the lies of the demons telling me the sermon will be a waste of time, the constant distractions, the heavy doubt, the sudden fatigue, and the uncharacteristic loss of memory. Once I identified it as spiritual warfare and started calling out the demons in the name of Jesus, the evening would proceed without incident, and I would be ready for the next morning.

There was the man in one of the places I served. One day, I made a visit to him, and we sat in his office. I could not get out of that place quick enough. I felt dirty the whole time I was in that room, and I made sure to pray for cleansing in Jesus's name as soon as I left.

Finally, there was the church in one of the places of little America that I served. I didn't enter that particular church all that much, but when I did, I suddenly felt uneasy. When I shared that feeling with a couple of others in the community, we all concluded that many years ago, demons had set up shop in that building and had been there for so long that the regular attenders of that church never noticed.

What do all these experiences have in common? They all occurred in little America. Those of us who live in little America are only sticking our heads in the sand if we think that combating demons in our little places is not necessary if we are going to win again.

So, how do we go about doing this? First, we need to understand what a demon is. Brian Burke, president of Wellsprings of Freedom International in Rock Island, Illinois, says that their leaders and team members use the (Greek) New Testament terminology for demons, sticking as close to the original language as possible in order to help Christians and churches to better understand the nature of spiritual warfare.

Therefore, the English word *demon* is a transliteration of the Greek nouns *daimon* or *daimonion*—two terms that are commonly used throughout the four gospels (see Matthew 8:31 and 12:24, 27, 28, and Mark 5:12). The word *daimon* occurs five times in the New Testament, while "daimonion" is used sixty times in the New Testament. These Greek words for demons are used interchangeably with the terms *unclean spirit* and *evil spirit*.

According to the prophecies told and information described in Isaiah 14:12–15 and Ezekiel 28:12–17, demons are simply "evil angels" or "fallen angels" who followed Satan and rose up in rebellion against God. Satan, as a created being, is portrayed in scripture as a fallen angel leading an army of fallen angels (demons). We gain another glimpse of this spiritual reality in Revelation 12:1–9 (NIV):

> The fifth angel sounded his trumpet, and I saw a star that had fallen from the sky to the earth. The star was given the key to the shaft of the Abyss. When he opened the Abyss, smoke rose from it like the smoke from a gigantic furnace. The sun and sky were darkened by the smoke from the Abyss. And out of the smoke locusts came down on the earth and were given power like that of scorpions of the earth. They were told not to harm the grass of the earth or any plant or tree, but only those people who did not have the seal of God on their foreheads. They were not allowed to kill them but only to torture them for five months. And the agony they suffered was like that of the sting of a scorpion when it strikes. During those days people will seek death but will not find it; they will long to die, but death will elude them.

> The locusts looked like horses prepared for battle. On their heads they wore something like crowns of gold, and their faces resembled human faces. Their hair was like women's hair, and their teeth were like lions' teeth. They had breastplates like breastplates of iron, and the sound of their wings was like the thundering of many horses and chariots rushing into battle.

To this very day, Satan and demons oppose Christ, the church, and the mission of Christ's kingdom on earth. They steal, kill, and destroy (John 10:10). They murder and lie (John 8:42–44). They deceive and distort the truth (2 Corinthians 11:3, 1 Timothy 4:1). They influence the way people behave (Ephesians 2:1–2). They tempt and seduce people into sin (Genesis 3:1–13, 4:6–7). And they accuse God's children (Zechariah 3:1–7, Revelation 12:10). (All verses are NIV.)

One of the problems we encounter when we venture into the spirit world and start talking about demons is that we do not understand the distinction between sinful behavior and demonic behavior, and thus we do not know whether we need to strive for the crucifixion of the sinful behavior or the exorcism of the demonic behavior.

For clarification on this matter I asked Brian Burke to send me an email with his thoughts on this. This is how he responded to my query:

> Within the ministry of Wellsprings of Freedom International, we believe there is a spiritual tension that exists between human sin and demonic influence. And we believe that *the truth* (what Scripture teaches) *is found in the tension.* In other words, there is a direct connection

between the two, but we can all too easily lean to one side/extreme or the other and get out of balance theologically. We do not believe that every problem in a person's life is caused by demons. Some problems are and some are not. Nor do we believe that every problem can be labeled by the church as a "sin problem" either. Often, it's a combination of both.

In fact, the Bible teaches that there are three spiritual enemies that war against our soul—*the world, the flesh, and the devil.* And these three forces work in conjunction with one another. Of course, Satan is behind all temptation and sin. We see this clearly in the Garden of Eden (Genesis 3) and in the accounts of Jesus' temptations in the wilderness (Matthew 4:1–11, Luke 4:1–13). And ever since the Fall (Genesis 1:1–13), we know that human beings are also born with a sin nature that naturally rebels against God and the things of God. Therefore, it is imperative to understand that Satan often works in cooperation with "the flesh" (and also the world system, its values, and beliefs, etc.) to intensify temptation and make it seemingly unbearable to resist.

How does this play out in the day-to-day experiences of church life? Here are a few situations I have run into. The first has to do with lying or dishonesty. There have been times when it has been clear to people at a meeting that certain decisions were made in a certain way and with definite wording only for the same participants to come back to a meeting the next month and completely deny things that were said, agreed upon, and even recorded from the last meeting. The normal reaction in that situation is to want to call out those people for lying. Sometimes that may be the case, but it can also be the case that twisting and blocking demonic spirits are at work, preventing the person in question from remembering how things actually went down at the previous meeting. Even if you can point to the minutes of the previous meeting to prove that what was decided was decided, the person/people in opposition will deny it.

Causing confusion and misunderstanding is one of the more common strategies that the devil uses to try to divide the church and createdisunity.

Another situation has to do with creating a negative or hostile environment. In this case, the devil sends out his demons of criticism, condemnation, and condescension. The result is that the atmosphere at the church is filled with negative comments, naysayers, Debbie downers, and glass-half-emptiers. The impact is that the church never gets anything done. Every new idea is doused. Every new dream is extinguished. Every new ministry is sabotaged. And the door to every new opportunity is slammed shut before anyone has the chance to go through it.

Another situation has to do with people who have gone through, or are going through, a difficult time in their life. The natural reaction of onlookers is to think these people will want to be in church because that is where they will get their support and encouragement. In many cases, just the opposite happens.

People going through difficult times often disappear from the church. Why? Because the devil has been lying to them. The devil and his minions are telling them that instead of being supported at church, they will be judged, that instead of being allowed to cry, they will be condemned as being weak for crying. At that point in their life, they want to keep a low profile, but the devil whispers to them that everyone will be looking at them when they come in and will be watching their step after they come in. The result is that hurting people stay away from the very people who could be helpers in healing the hurt.

Another situation occurs because of a lack of forgiveness. When I say this, it is not because others will not forgive us but because we do not forgive ourselves. So often I have heard people say they cannot forgive themselves for something they have done. While they know that God forgives sin and while they have experienced forgiveness from others, they live under the weight of condemnation because the devil has convinced them that they are still a terrible person. The result is the people are held in bondage because they feel they can never crawl out from under the cover of their guilt. Every time they look in the mirror, the devil places a label above them that says, "Guilty!" Because of the work of the devil, these people never feel worthy or qualified to serve the Lord in any capacity.

In these ways and more, the devil keeps his grip on the hands of the church and his foot on the heart of the church, and the church, instead of going out and making disciples, stays inwardly focused.

For the church in little America, and big America as well, to win, we need to pray in the name of Jesus Christ against the warfare led by Satan. We do that by praying for the discernment to identify the demons that are warring against our people and our communities. There are many resources on the internet to help us make those identifications.

Once we discern the demons we are fighting against, we need to pray aloud and with boldness. Demons cannot read our minds, but they do understand our words. If someone is trying to steal from you, being polite is probably not the best tactic to use. When people are out to take what belongs to us, being bold is the best way to go. Being bold lets the attacker know we mean business, that we are not afraid of them, and that we expect them to bow to our wishes. It is the same idea when we speak to Satan and his demons.

As we pray, we must always invoke the name of Jesus. Scripture is clear that demons do not shudder and submit to our names, but they do submit to the name. It is the name of Jesus that grabs their attention and gains their submission. They know that Jesus is more powerful than they are, and they know that when Jesus is involved in the fight, they don't have a chance. The way to make that clear is to continually use the name of Jesus in the fight.

When we are praying in the name of Jesus with boldness, it is also very fitting that we tell the demons that there are not to be any manifestations from them. Many of us have heard the stories of demons making a big scene when they are being exorcised. The way to eliminate those scenes and prevent any personal injury is simply to tell the demons that they cannot act out. Remember, demons will submit to the name of Jesus, and they know the punishment Jesus can and will inflict on them when they fail to give in. It is certainly appropriate to lay down all the ground rules to the demons when we are fighting against them.

There are instances where a team is so superior to the opponent that coming up with a game plan is unnecessary. There are times when the opponent is so inferior that we can do whatever we want, and we will win or, if we are the inferior ones, we will lose. I have been a part of those situations as both a player and a coach. There were basketball games we went into in high school that we knew we would not win even if our coach had the best game plan ever devised. There were games I coached for my daughter's soccer team that I knew that we were going to win no matter what how poor of a game plan I concocted and games we were going to lose no matter how good of a game plan I concocted.

But when it comes to the kingdom of God and the church winning again in little America, this is not the situation. The truth is that whether we win will be determined not only by how we game plan for our strengths but also how we game plan for the strengths of the opponent. The outcome of the game is so important that we cannot just roll out the ball and wait to see what happens.

A LITTLE PEP TALK

Anyone who has ever played sports and taken the game they played seriously has dreamed of finishing the game as the hero. We dream of being the one who hits the home run in the bottom of the ninth inning that ends the game as we jump on home plate amid the throng of jubilant teammates hitting us on the top of the head. We dream of being the one who hits the game-winning shot just as the buzzer sounds in basketball. We dream of being the one who sinks the twenty-foot putt on the final hole, the one who catches the pass in the end zone, the one who scores the go-ahead goal in sudden-death overtime. These are the moments that drive us to train and practice and train and practice and train and practice until we think we cannot train and practice for another minute. These are the moments that make all the pain of the preceding months and years worth the effort. These are the moments that keep us from walking away, that keep us from staying in bed, that keep us from the fast-food restaurants, and that keep us from throwing in the towel after repeated failure.

It was a dream like this that kept me plugging away on this book. Until I stopped. The dream was to be able to finish this book on a high note, with a grand-slam home run, with a long birdie putt, with a three-pointer from half-court, with a shot that hit the back of the net just as the red light went on.

The dream was to conclude with a pep talk that would inspire people to get out of their seats and into the world as pioneers in their community, reinvigorating the floundering churches in their community with one disciple group after another. It was going to be such a great moment. It was going to be the pep talk that made "win one for the Gipper" a moment of silence in comparison to the crescendo of "win one for the church in little America." It was going to be the pep talk that would erase all apathy and douse all discouragement. It was going to be the pep talk that would restart aborted revivals and refresh sleepy saints. Until it was not.

What is the little pep talk for the church in little America? Do not give up. Do not quit. Do not surrender. Do not compromise. Do not beat yourselves up. Do not lose hope. Playing a game involves a lot of losing. The last college basketball team to go undefeated was the 1976 Indiana Hoosiers. The last National Football League team to go undefeated was the 1972 Miami Dolphins. The last pro basketball team or baseball team or hockey team to go undefeated was never. The last baseball player to only make an out six out of ten times was Ted Williams in 1941 when he hit .406. Every player every year strikes out from time to time in baseball. Every player every year misses a shot from time to time in basketball and hockey and soccer. Every player every year makes a few bogeys or worse in golf. Every player every year misses a tackle or drops a pass or throws an interception in football.

Failure is part of the game in sports, and failure is part of the game in building the kingdom of God. We want to have everyone fired up about making disciples. A majority never will. We want to have everyone involved in a life group or discipleship group. A majority never will. We want to have everyone sharing his or her faith. A majority never will. We want to have everyone ministering to others. A majority never will. We want to have everyone connecting with others. A majority never will. We want everyone to be straining for the goal line. A majority will always be content to play the game at the fifty-yard line. We want everyone to be encouragers. There will be always be complainers. We want everyone to acknowledge the devil and engage in battle against him. A majority never will.

So, what do we do? Do we just give up? Do we tank with the hope of getting a better draft choice? Do we lower the expectations so that we are happy to just tread water? Do we spend all our time and energy oiling the squeaky wheels? Do we go back to singing "Kumbaya" because the tune is familiar, and the atmosphere is comfortable?

The answer to all these questions is a resounding *no*. If the church in little America is going to start winning again, we need to be faithful and obedient. We may not have the adrenaline rushes of hitting a walk-off home run or making a game-winning shot, but we can have the satisfaction of small victories and the honor of hearing God saying to us, "Job well done."

When Jesus started his ministry, he didn't start with the majority. Rather he started with twelve, and twelve was more than enough. If we are going to win again, we need to be willing to start not with what we wish we had but with what we do have. Many churches are seeing their numbers decline at an alarming rate through the pandemic. If we are going to win, we may have to recalculate what we have to work with and pump our energy into that number. The truth is we may not even need twelve to start winning again. It can very well be two or four or eight.

When Paul started his ministry, he didn't start with the support of the majority. Rather, he started with the support of Ananias and Barnabas. He started with two people who came to his side, believed in him, and paved the way so he could make inroads with his doubters and critics. He did not have a large support group, but think of how his story may have ended without Ananias and Barnabas.

The church in little America is not going to start winning again because of the size of the dog in the fight but because of the size of the fight in the dog. The church in little America will start winning again when there are a few devoted disciples of Jesus who are committed to getting on their knees in prayer and then getting together with a couple of other devoted disciples and combining their resources, vision, and passion. Kurt Kaiser nailed it in his song "Pass It On": "It only takes a spark to get a fire going, and soon all those around will warm up to its glowing."

We need to remember that winning is not determined by butts, bucks, and buildings but by connecting, sharing, and ministering. Whether you are a church board reading this, a pastor reading this, or a layperson reading this, know that winning again does not depend on the size of the team but on a couple of players who buy into what our coach, Jesus Christ, said and did and start executing his game plan.

During Advent, I took a closer look at the wise men. I did not realize there was so much we did not know about them. Bible scholars have different opinions on their backgrounds, on where they came from, on how many of them there were, on how long it took them to get to Jesus, on what their mode of transportation was, and on how much gold, frankincense, and myrrh they brought. But with all the things we do not know for sure, everyone agrees on this truth: they eventually got there. Though the journey was long and though the journey was difficult and though the journey was sometimes uncertain, they never quit; they never stopped going forward. Even when they knew King Herod was trying to play them, they didn't allow the opposition to stop them. The wise men are but one example of many in the Bible of people who ended up making a difference because they would not quit.

I finish with a little bit of baseball trivia. Ready for a baseball trivia question? Who is Clint Courtney? If you are unsure, do not bother requesting the answer from Cooperstown, New York. Clint never came close to making it into the Baseball Hall of Fame. In fact, it is very doubtful that his picture appeared on any bubble gum cards. This guy was not a legend in his own time—not even in his own mind. He was only a memory maker for his family and a few die-hard fans who were inspired by his tremendous fortitude. Clint played catcher for the Baltimore Orioles in the 1950s. During his career, he earned the nickname of Scrap Iron, implying that he was hard, weathered, and tough. Old Scrap broke no records—only bones. He had little power or speed on the base paths. As for grace and style, he made the easiest play look rather difficult. But armed with mitt and mask, Scrap Iron never flinched from any challenge.

Batters often missed the ball and caught his shin. Their foul tips nipped his elbow. Runners fiercely plowed into him, spikes first, as he defended home plate. Though often doubled over in agony and flattened in a heap of dust, Clint Courtney never quit. Invariably, he would slowly get up, shake off the dust, punch the pocket of his mitt once or twice, and nod to his pitcher to throw another one. The game would go on and Courtney with it—scarred, bruised, clutching his arm in pain, but determined to continue. He resembled a POW with tape, splints, braces, and other kinds of paraphernalia that wounded people wear. Some made fun of him, calling him a masochist. Insane. Others remember him as a true champion.

How is the church in little America going to win again? It is going to win again with the Clint Courtneys of the local church. It is going to win with people who will not flinch in the face of any challenge the church will face. It is going to win with people who will get hit on their elbows with foul balls, hit on their shins with baseball bats, and plowed into while guarding the faith but never give up, always getting back on their feet and nodding for God to throw the next pitch. It is going to win with people who are scarred, bruised, and clutching our hearts in pain but determined to continue.

It is not the heroes' ending I wanted and probably not the heroes' ending you wanted either. What it is is reality. Building the kingdom is hard work. Every once in a while, a victory is attained in a grand fashion, but more often than not, the victory comes through bumps and bruises and scratches and scars. Still, as Clint Courtney proved, as long as we stay in the game, there is hope, and when we persevere, God regards us as true champions.

SMALL GROUP DISCUSSION QUESTIONS

Chapter 1—Too Little Repentance

Critique can be hard to take. The author put before us the importance of approaching God with a "broken and contrite heart. Do you sense your church family needing this kind of a heart? And if so, in what formats may it be offered in lieu of not having a specific time in your church family's life to do so (individually and corporately)?

The author then listed five areas in which we could consider confessing our sins as a church today. Would you agree with these? And as you think of your church, are their ones that rise to the top? Can you talk about them? What might be the hardest ones to confess? Would you add any to these? What might be a good way for your church to address these?

Chapter 2—Too Little God

Surviving versus thriving—how do you see this tension in little America? How do you see this in the church in little America?

Too little God? Does this resonate with what you see at the church in little America? And if so, how do you see it in areas that agree with this chapter? Do you see it being exhibited in other ways?

How might the church look in our communities with a bigger God? (Yes, do a little dreaming!)

Chapter 3—Too Little Hope

In little America's church, do you sense this fading of hope? And if so, in what ways has it been showing up?

Can you remember times in your church's history when hope seemed alive? What was happening? What would you attribute it to? That is, what was working in a way that a sense of hope was prevalent?

What do you think might be factors/circumstances in the church, our community, and our world that may be challenging hope?

Chapter 4—Too Little Cooperation

What do you think have been contributing factors that have so many churches in little America that do not (or will not) work together?

What about secondary issues?

Fill in the blank (and be ready to talk about your answer).

I could never cooperate with someone from another church if they believed _____.

Does theology often crush cooperation? Give examples.

Have you seen these cooperation crushers in play in your town or church? Give examples.

Chapter 5—Too Little Focus

Kumbaya! (Feel-good moments)
Can you give some examples of these moments that can take individuals and churches off focus? (If you can give specific examples from your own experience or your church's, that would be great!) Why are we so drawn to these kumbaya experiences? How and why has the church gravitated toward this?

Caring (intentionally)
Seems hard to say that this can take us off focus … Explain how you see it happening. How well do you as a church take on this role of caring? If we were to expand our idea of what true caring encompasses, what would caring then look like? Why do we seem to shy away from taking care into our neighborhoods, workplaces, and so on?

Education
In what ways has education become a stumbling block for focus in our lives and in the lives of our churches? Try to be specific and include things from your own experience in your life and that of your church as you are comfortable sharing. Might education in our churches set up class structures in our church

families? And if so, how might it further damage application over knowledge?

Chapter 6—Too Little Impact

Are you surprised by any of the findings in this section? If so which and why?

The author asked a few times, "What is the church in little America to do?" What ideas can you come up with to answer that? Where might it start? (Because it seems like it will not happen with sweeping change but come from a process.)

What other areas in our church and personal ministries do we see that we might need to give up to focus them more on God?

A Little Strategy!

What does winning look like for your church today? Where are the wins coming from?

Can you describe the difference between being a disciple and being a Christian? Why do you feel there is a difference?

How do you keep score at your church? What are the things that your church pays the most attention to? What might be some changes you would suggest for that scoreboard?

Like the woman in the textile mill who did not check with the foreman, how do we do with going to God? Your church? Your leaders? In your personal life?

What has been your experience with spiritual warfare in your walk with God? When has spiritual warfare been emphasized in churches that you have been a part of?

What are some instances where you can see that the battle against the devil was a bigger issue than the battle against the flesh?

A Little Pep Talk

What dreams have you entertained about being a "hero" in something you were involved in?

If you were given the assignment of giving a pep talk to your church, what would you say?

Give some more examples of characters in the Bible succeeding because they did not give up.

How does the story of Clint Courtney resonate with you and your service for the Lord?

What are the first steps that you feel you need to take after reading this book?

Printed in the United States
by Baker & Taylor Publisher Services